High

&

TRACTOR
WHEELS

High Heels & TRACTOR WHEELS

Copyright © 2017 by Brianna Walker

ISBN-13:
978-1543287509

ISBN-10:
1543287506

Give feedback on the book at:
farmersfate@agritimesnw.com

Printed in U.S.A

Dedicated To:
my grandmother, who encouraged my writing
my sweetheart, who puts up with my writing

Farmer's Fate

Shopping

Breakdowns & Accidents

Farm Girls

Surprises & Adventures

Home & Gardening

Family

Politics

Traveling

Holidays

Weather & Water

Dating & Marriage

Animals & Pets

Kids

Life & Death

Farmer's Fate

Farmer = Someone who thinks a 40 hour
work week is an after-school job

Fate = our free will + God's free will

So you think you can farm?

*Y*ou've seen farmers with flexible winter schedules and envied their 'bossless' careers—but before you give up your 9-5, take the following tests to see if farming is the right occupation for you.

CLOTHING TEST: Look through your closet and throw away anything that has an expensive-sounding name. Lay the rest in the driveway and after dumping a couple buckets of dirt over them—drive on them a few times to make sure the dirt is well ground in. If there are still clothes that remain hole-free, squirt some battery acid on them. Make sure all your hats have local farm business logos on them.

MONEY TEST: Go to the nearest bank. Set your wallet on the counter and ask the clerk to help himself. Now proceed to the nearest farm equipment store. Go to the head office and arrange for your income to be directly deposited to their store. Take out a loan to pay taxes to Uncle Sam. Then practice begging in the mirror in preparation for asking your loan officer for next year's operator loan.

FEEDING TEST: Get up at 5 a.m. to start the water on your yard. Look at your watch at 10 and realize you haven't eaten, but you're too busy now. At 2:30 you make a flying trip to Taco Bell. You have just taken a bite, when your phone rings: a tractor tire blew and there's calcium all over the road. The police on the scene are demanding you clean it up now. You set down your taco to take care of the emergency. Four hours later you realize the dog ate it. You find an old bag of peanuts behind the seat in the tractor and eat the last 6. Add to that a mini candy bar and two packets of hot sauce you found in the jockeybox.

SLEEP TEST: Stay up until nearly 11 p.m. finishing projects for the next day. Then set your alarm for 2:30 a.m. Go out and check the lawn for moisture. If it's too dry, go back to bed and set your alarm for 3:30 a.m. Continue this every hour until the lawn is the correct moisture, then dress quickly. You are now up for the rest of the day. Repeat until the summer is over.

SOCIAL TEST: Decline any social invitation from April to November. It's farming season. If you do happen to have free time, you'd rather sleep.

PHYSICAL TEST: Spend 5 hours a day lifting and walking with a 40-foot sprinkler pipe. Try this in thick mud. Windy days work well too.

FINAL ASSIGNMENT: Find someone who already farms. Lecture them on how they can improve their tillage practices, water efficiency, and soil erosion. Emphasize how much better organic farming is to the environment. Suggest ways they can go green. Enjoy this experience. It will be the last time you will have all the answers (or the time to share them.)

Makes you wonder...

$\mathcal{D}$uring lunch on a recent school field trip, some of us chaperones began chatting with some parents. I began visiting with a well-dressed mother of three boys.

We started talking about the purpose of the trip—introducing middle school students to colleges with the hope that they would eventually pursue higher education.

While we both agreed on the merits of attending college, I was shocked at the way she had persuaded her older children.

She blithely told me about lining up jobs for her kids with a local apple grower. I nodded approvingly—at first. They were to work in a packing house, filling boxes. She smiled broadly and became more animated just before she dropped her bombshell. When her kids came home that day—exhausted, she sat them down and explained to them that if they didn't go to college they would be stuck working in agriculture.

They certainly didn't want that to happen—right? I was still smiling politely, even though her comments ruffled my feathers. "—so I called the apple grower and told them my kids weren't coming back." She sat back as if waiting for praise on the glorious scheme she cooked up to ensure her kids attended college. I had to bite my tongue—hard!

I didn't know which was worse: leaving the farmer minus two employees at the drop of a hat? Or teaching your kids that they are above sweat and hard work?

What was wrong with teaching them the value of a dollar? About great work ethics? And we wonder what's wrong with kids these days?

Botanicals:
Your fern is on line one

A symphony orchestra plays before a hushed audience. Suddenly the shrill ring of a phone cuts across the concert hall. A rude but typical interruption—right? Today perhaps, but the year is 1965. A dark haired man rises from his seat and walks quickly to the lobby where he seeks refuge in a broom closet. There he removes his ringing shoe—the precursor to the modern cell phone. It was probably the first time a phone went off in an audience—but it will never be the last. Get Smart's shoe phone, however far-fetched it once seemed, is fast becoming ancient history. After all, it was a rotary phone.

What was science fiction 30 years ago has long since become commonplace. The first cellphone came to market in 1984. A Motorola DynaTac 8000X, weighing 2 pounds and selling for $3,995. That Flintstone relic would never be mistaken for the sleek 3 ounce Razor of today.

As the price decreased, it seems like everyone bought into this Get Smart gadget: from the elementary school kid to the senior citizen.

And the days when phones were used exclusively for talking are over—now phones seemed to be used more for apps, GPS, social media, Netflix, games and texting, than just regular old talking.

China now sells a cellphone that can puff out a scent. It's like a ring tone, except more of a smell tone. Your girlfriend calls and you get a whiff of perfume. If John Deere gets its hands on this technology and combines it with GPS you might drive through town and get a whiff of that new diesel engine and directions to the nearest dealership.

Recently, the *Korea Times* reported that Samsung is working with South Korean scientists to develop "living" cellphones that can "feel, think, evolve and reproduce." "A three dimensional avatar will lurk inside the cellphone and adjust itself to characteristics of the cellphone carriers." The *Korea Times* reports "Its personality can get better or worse depending on how people treat it." Ahhhhhh, I just want a phone I can talk into—not something I have to keep happy! What happens if I get a prissy one that doesn't like sitting in a dirty combine all day?

This is starting to look like life in the Jetson's household; after all they had the VisaPhone which is similar to the new video phones. But even in their futuristic world, plants didn't use cellphones.

A project at New York University helps plants call for help if they're parched or over-watered. Moisture sensors send a signal over a wireless network using human voices to send messages of need or thanks directly to your cellphone. Great. Now I have to screen telemarketers, ex-boyfriends, and my houseplants??

The nod

It has recently been brought to my attention that I am rude when it comes to acknowledging people while driving. I was shocked to learn that I make little or no attempt to motion or acknowledge people when they wave at me. I was sure this must be a mistake, but it did make me consciously aware of my motions. Which brought me to a startling realization—I don't wave.

Different people have different ways of showing recognition while they are driving. One older gentleman near my parent's home always gives a smart salute to passing motorists, while my father-in-law gives a full up-and-down wrist wave. One of my uncles would give half-an-index-finger wave—although one time he lifted two fingers completely off the steering wheel—I figured he must have won the lottery!

Motorcyclists have their own version of waving: lifting the left arm out to the side of the bike, open palm fingers outstretched. Snowmobilers raise their right fist, fingers upraised to denote the number of riders behind them. Cowboys tip their hats, and Californian's give you the birdie.

Farmers also have their own brand of acknowledgment... the Nod. Driving machinery down the road, one hand on the throttle and the other on the wheel, watching for mailboxes, garbage cans and passing cars, leaves a rare opportunity to raise a hand in greeting. Thus the Nod is born. Passing farmers and ranchers will notice the nearly imperceptible Nod and return it with one of their own.

Growing up pitching melons, if we were to wave at passing friends, it was likely we'd get a 20-pound melon in the gut—which makes the Nod incredibly practical. Each one of my siblings grew up inherently learning the Nod. Now, even if we're passengers in the car, and a friend pulls up beside us, chances are we will nod our heads in acknowledgment.

This isn't rude, or lacking in social etiquette, it's just common sense down on the farm. If you want acknowledgment, look for the Nod; if you want a wave, try the ocean.

You need a Power Stroke for what?

*F*irewood, watermelons or hay: it didn't seem to matter what we were loading, the pickup was never fully loaded until the back-end was squatting and the tires were beginning to bulge—then it was full. We assumed as long as there was space, you should keep loading—no point in hauling a half empty pickup.

The older I get, the more I realize how that hauling perspective didn't spread to many outside of agriculture. We recently were hauling some four-wheelers to the mountains for a weekend of fun. We asked some friends to haul two in a little ATV trailer behind their pickup. Before agreeing, they had to check the owner's manual to see how much weight their pickup could tow. What?

And it's not specific to them...someone else we're acquainted with just bought a little camp trailer—and before he would tow it he removed the performance chip in his pickup—he was afraid it would get too hot. We've also had several people come to buy hay, and they believe a half-ton pickup means it will haul half a ton...with that mentality it would take forever to haul anything!

But the one that really left us scratching our heads was last weekend. We watched two people loading a fair-sized dinghy onto a trailer and then they pulled the both the dinghy and the trailer out of the boat launch by hand! We watched, mesmerized, as they pulled their trailer into the parking lot, parked it, then walked away. We were still chuckling about it, when a big diesel, one-ton dually with a back-window decal reading "More Power," backed down the boat ramp. Our attention strayed for a bit, but was immediately captured again when the pickup drove past us pulling a rowboat no more than 6 feet long...smaller than the one pulled out by hand.

Recently, I followed an old beat-up Ford Escort through the McDonald's drive-thru. The back window sported a huge Peterbilt logo decal. I wonder what the owner's manual specs are on that vehicle? No matter, it could have pulled up the rowboat with minimal tire bulging—with or without a performance chip!

Country road etiquette

"**W**ho was that?"

"I don't know," our neighbor answered his wife. "But I see the vehicle all the time."

"So why would you wave at someone just because you recognize the vehicle?" she questioned.

"Because that's just what you do on country roads..."

Later on that same neighbor was the recipient of that same country road etiquette. He happened to have a flat tire on that same road—over a dozen people stopped to offer assistance. Not because they knew him...but they 'recognized the vehicle.'

That's the joy of living in the country. But recently, the city has been encroaching on those country roads—bringing with them their loud horns and waving fingers.

I understand wanting to breathe country air, smell mint in the air during harvest and see baby lambs playing king of the mountain—that's why I don't live in the city. But it seems that many people move into rural areas for the pastoral views—and forget what it takes to get them that way.

Earlier this summer we had a run-in with a guy who said he didn't move out to the country to have someone farm next to his property. Say that again?

I was recently flagging a combine up a hill on a narrow two-lane road with steep banks on either side. There was no room to pass—even if it had been a passing zone—which it wasn't.

That fact didn't seem to dissuade a certain orange pickup. He swerved one way and then the other, trying to find a gap big enough to squeeze through. We had barely topped the hill, when he peeled out into a bordering alfalfa field, making damaging tracks as his back end skidded back and forth trying to get enough traction in the wet field to get back on the road.

After mucking up the field, he pulled back in front of the combine, and laid on the horn as he swerved around me holding up his finger so as to be sure I wouldn't miss it.

The pickup was barely out of sight, when we met another car. It slows down and pulls over, as does a pickup with a trailer. Just then, another car barrels down the road. It pulls around the parked cars and my flashing lights and rolls through the intersection and right into the oncoming header of the combine. What are people thinking? How can you miss the flagger cars or the 22-foot-wide combine with flashers blinking?

I believe that some people really don't know to pull over in wide spots, or that mailboxes, garbage cans and fences can make passing them even more difficult. Then there are people that seem to be (in the words of a friend) "dumb as a cedar fence post."

So next time you're in a hurry for dinner, and you pull in behind a slow-moving pea harvester, before you lay on the horn, remember your dinner came in part from another slow-moving vehicle. Take a deep breath, and as you drive around them, give them a five-finger wave, because, 'that's just what you do on a country road.'

Picking out a watermelon

*P*icking out a "good melon" is not an exact science. In fact, I believe there are as many theories about choosing melons as there are regarding the chicken and the egg.

I have named three of the more classic melon-picking approaches. There is the Nail Scratch in which someone drags their fingernail across the top of the rind. I'm still trying to figure out how a scratch on a melon and green peel under their nail will determine if the melon is good.

But then what do I know? Growing up with a melon box as a playpen, and a pocketknife for a baby spoon doesn't mean I know how to pick a good melon—or does it?

Second, there is the Fist Thumping technique. People will lean close to the melon and pound it repeatedly. Some people do this with confidence, while others knock just because they've seen other people do it. Few people seem to know what they're thumping for.

The Bee Sting approach involves looking for rough brown spots that often leak a sort of sticky pitch. This is a theory that believes a bee will sting only the sweet melons. Since the majority of melons lack these spots, does that mean only a small percentage of melons are sweet, or is the bee population just too small?

One afternoon a stylish lady stopped by and wanted a watermelon. She pulled two drinking straws out of her purse and proceeded to "water-witch" the watermelons. I've always wondered if her method really worked. It would be kind of funny to see the melon pickers carrying drinking straws—although I'm afraid it wouldn't be very time efficient.

Other people push, poke, sniff and shake the melons. One person recently told me they wouldn't buy a melon without a long stem on it. (I had thought a long stem meant someone needed a new knife.)

Now that we've discussed several methods, what is the best way to pick out a melon? Is it the Nail Scratch, the Fist Thump, the Bee Sting, all of the above, or none of the above?

While contemplating how best to explain, I began thinking of pasta. The Italians are to pasta, what Hermiston is to watermelons. And while the Italians are very willing to share their food, I've never heard of them volunteering family recipes. So I decided to keep the secret safe, but I will give you directions to our melon farm if you still want a good watermelon.

Good news, bad news

$\mathcal{G}$ood News: You got most of your ripping finished today.

Bad News: You unburied a concrete culvert in the process.

Good News: The city council voted you Farmer of the Year.

Bad News: The vote passed 31-30.

Good News: The Water Board accepted your job description the way you wrote it.

Bad News: They were so inspired by it, they also formed a search committee to find somebody capable of filling the position.

Good News: You finally found a farm manager who approaches things exactly the same way you do.

Bad News: The farm mutinied.

Good News: Mrs. Jones is wild about your fresh produce.

Bad News: Mrs. Jones is also wild about head cheese,

blubber and camels' feet.

Good News: Employee morale rose dramatically the last three weeks.

Bad News: You were on vacation.

Good News: Your biggest critic just left your town.

Bad News: He has been appointed the DEQ's head inspector for your county.

Good News: You paid off your operating loan, so you get to do it all over again.

Bad News: You paid off your operating loan, so you get to do it all over again!

Days of our lives...

$\mathcal{A}$nyone who farms, or is married to a farmer knows about 'winter projects.' You can think of them like desserts... often desired....but unneeded in sustaining the body. Many projects fall under this category. It seems to be a catchall for things that need done but don't generate income.

In the summer, when harvest is in full swing, it is understandable why some projects are impractical. Replacing the window broken from a neighbor's stray bullet, fixing the bathroom sink that only has cold water, hanging the closet door that has been missing for 6 years, re-roofing the hen house, and putting lights in the shop...while all would be nice, none is imperative to harvest.

As the summer heat turns to autumn breezes, I get excited knowing we will soon tackle another item on the ever growing list of 'winter projects.'

This winter it was my kitchen. We replaced our old black 1950s vintage cabinets with 'new to me' white ones encased in diamond plating. The project started out well enough, but after enough of the kitchen was replaced so cooking became possible (though difficult because the sink was on the deck), the sunshine broke through the winter cloud cover. This brought on a bad case of spring fever in my husband.

Each morning the sun glistened on our breakfast dishes and I heard: "Well since it's nice out, I think I'm going to get some more field work done."

Meanwhile my kitchen remained packed in boxes in our son's room. I actually smiled to see the sun replaced by big raindrops—finally a day to work on the kitchen! The thought had barely formed when I heard my husband say: "Well it looks like it's gonna rain all day. It'll be a good day to fix fence."

The next day when the wind picked up, I heard: "Well it's too windy to spray...guess it'll be a good day to work in the shop." For lunch that day, my husband was surprised when I served him food on a paper plate with a plastic fork. I met his questioning look with a gesture at the hole where the sink should be and wires hanging from the ceiling where the light should be.

"If a sunny day means field work, a rainy day means fixing fence, and a windy day is a shop day...what kind of day is a kitchen-fixing day?"

He shrugged, "A red letter day?"

20 laws of farming

1. The fuel filter you must special order today will go on an overstock sale next week.

2. Spill-proof coffee mugs — will.

3. The chances of a glob of grease falling off a zirc is directly proportional to the proximity of your bank loan officer's expensive loafer.

4. If you happen to have the service truck in the field at the time of an unexpected breakdown...hold off on the congratulatory dance...it's probably metric.

5. The nicer the jacket is you took off in the tractor, the greater the chance of it winding up behind the seat for the remainder of the winter.

6. Common items we use daily will slide themselves to the back and bottom of the toolbox, while things like the broken pair of pliers and the rusty pipe wrench always manage to be on top.

7. The chance your neighbor will drive by dramatically increases when you shear a bolt or plug the swather, or feed a piece of forgotten handline into the header of the combine.

8. Tell a man there are 300 million wheat stalks in your field and he'll believe you. Tell him the tractor hood has just been painted and he'll have to touch it to be sure.

9. The legibility of an invoice is inversely proportional to its importance.

10. If you borrow the neighbor's ladder to trim your trees, be sure a branch will fall in such a way as to bend the ladder—before it knocks you to the ground.

11. A dropped power tool will always land on the concrete instead of the soft ground—unless it's running, in which case it will fall on something it can damage (like your foot).

12. The gooey mud that adds 10 pounds to your rubber boots while changing handline, will immediately fall off the moment you step onto the floorboards of your pickup.

13. 1 washer + 1 dryer + 2 expensive wool socks = 1 wool sock + 1 grumpy husband.

14. The probability of rain is directly proportional to the amount of fence that has to be fixed.

15. The more important it is to get to the Napa store, the greater the chance they closed early.

16. An oil plug dropped into the oil pan will relocate to maximize splash.

17. Machinery will be damaged in direct proportion to its value.

18. The chances of blowing a tire are inversely proportional to the proximity of a tire company.

19. If a tire decides to blow, it won't be the tire you have a spare for, it will instead be the tire that comes with the biggest price tag.

20. The greater the value of your guest's car, the greater the probability that the chickens will roost on it.

I think these "Laws" are some of the reasons farmers tend to carry duct tape, and baler twine, and if that fails…a big hammer....

An extra hour of sleep

*W*e all participate in an odd tradition of messing with time in an attempt to gain an hour of daylight. An old timer when asked once about Daylight Saving Time answered: "Only the government would believe that you could cut a foot off the top of a blanket, sew it on the bottom, and have a longer blanket."

Yet most Americans continue to perpetuate this interesting ritual in saving time. Although since no daylight is actually saved, Daylight Shifting Time would be better, or perhaps Daylight Time Shifting, though neither sounds politically desirable, and that's what it seems to boil down to—political desirability.

I've always heard it said DST gives you more daylight during working hours which potentially cuts down energy costs and allows for more time to be spent outside.

Recent studies seem to be debunking the energy-saving theory. One study in Indiana actually concluded it raised the total household income in the state by $9 million. Another in California saw no discernible shift in energy consumption at all.

Jay Leno once addressed a second theory that DST gives farmers more daylight hours...well if there are only 8 hours of daylight...then there are only 8 hours of daylight...it doesn't matter how they correspond to the numbers on a clock. And if clock hours mattered to anyone, I'd think farmers would be way down on the list.

As one rancher commented: "My animals get hungry at dawn, whether that comes at 5 a.m. or 8 a.m." Most farmers rise at dawn and go to bed when they're too tired to keep working, or their tractor quits or the cow dies, whichever comes last.

So if it doesn't seem to save noticeable energy, and farmers and ranchers don't benefit from it...then who does? In 1984 *Fortune* magazine estimated that a 7-week extension of DST would yield an additional $30 million for 7-Eleven stores and the National Golf Foundation estimated the extension would increase golf industry revenues $200-300 million. Interesting, huh?

Despite the lack of reasons for DST, I really have no objections...I only object to the implication that I am wasting something valuable if I stay in bed after the sun has risen. Perhaps I am an admirer of moonlight, and DST reduces my time for enjoying it!

To Benjamin Franklin's "early to bed, and early to rise, makes one healthy, wealthy and wise," I retort: "early to rise and early to bed, makes one healthy, wealthy and dead—(tired that is)."

Corn gender

*W*e considered snipe hunting, but seeing how exhausted they all looked as they dragged themselves from the car, we settled for a nice visit instead. Our unexpected guests had just arrived from Oklahoma, and seemed pleased to be out of the vehicle.

It's always fun to visit with long-lost relatives, and the ladies and I were deep in conversation before we noticed the "men-folk" had gravitated toward the machinery—catching up is never as exciting as drooling over farm machinery.

We practically had the world's problems solved before they came strolling back, touting a *Fastline* and *Tractor-house* under each arm.

The rest of the evening's conversation revolved around the pros and cons of red vs. green paint. Thankfully the sun went down quickly, darkening all shades and colors of tractors and equipment.

Too soon, morning arrived, and the men took off for a trip through the fields. My husband eagerly showed his fields to our farm-hungry cousin who seemed to eat it up. They stopped at a cornfield, and our cousin inquired why the rows were varied heights.

"The taller rows are females," my husband explained, "we can't plant the males until they've reached a certain number of heat units." He continued on with his mini corn lesson while the cousin looked curiously at the field.

"I didn't know there was male and female corn," he finally said. "How do you tell it apart?" My cousin laughed, "Do you look under the tassels?"

My husband suddenly envisioned a snipe hunt. He turned and with a deadpan expression asked, "You ever hear of corn nuts?"

You know you're a farmer when...

'You know you are a farmer...when you go to the tractor on laundry day to get your dirty clothes,' I typed into my status update on my facebook page. I hit enter, pleased with my wit for the day, and scooped up my armload of clothes. As the days turned chilly, I'd begun looking for the jackets and shirts that I'd worn in the spring. After a fruitless trip to the closet, I made a machinery round. Between the swather, the combine, and the tractors, I found 4 of my shirts, 7 of my husband's shirts, and 3 unclaimed jackets that will make nice additions to my closet.

Later that evening I checked my facebook page again, and was seriously surprised with the comments my post had drawn.

"Why did you take your clothes off in the tractor?"

"Some type of farmer activity I am not familiar with?"

"Maybe those are questions best left unasked."

Successive comments made me blush deep red. My innocently funny post had become terribly suggestive. I was beginning to think about deleting it when I saw my grandma's comment. "So true!! Grandpa was looking for a warm work shirt the other morning, none in his closet. I found one behind the seat of his pick-up, one hanging on a fence post by the barn, and several in the garage. He needs to check the tractors and the swather."

Farmers may have dirty nails, tattered clothes, and old vehicles—but they've got to have some of the most expensive (and highly attractive) clothes hampers I've ever seen.

As I continued putting together my "you know you're a farmer list, I thought better of posting it on facebook, and instead decided my *Agri-Times NW* readers would enjoy them more (or at least understand them).

You know you're a farmer when...
• Your dog rides with you more than your spouse.
• You convince your spouse that an overnight, out-of-state trip for equipment parts is a vacation.
• You wear your Muck boots for every activity except church.
• You've never thrown away a 5-gallon bucket.
• You have used baler twine to attach a license plate.
• You have used a chainsaw to remodel your house.
• You remember the seed population and yields on a farm you rented 10 years ago, but cannot recall the age of your children.
• You have driven off the road while examining your neighbors' crops or checking out their new machinery.
• Your alfalfa field is cut shorter than your lawn.
• You've used the same knife to cut baler twine, the ends off grease tubes, take the sticker out of the dog's paw, castrate, and eat watermelon....

Bipolar balers & warm milk

"So why would you grow straw and not wheat?" my passenger asked as I baled up some wheat straw. Thankfully I'd already swallowed my Gatorade. I snorted a giggle before I turned to see sincerity written on her face.

This was not some naive inner city kid sitting beside me, instead she was a well-educated teacher who had attended high school in the foothills of wheat country, and now lived in my small rural town. She had brought her daughter and step-grandkids out to experience "farm life" and "big tractors." After explaining that straw is just a part of the wheat stalk, she expressed amazement that straw was not a crop of its own, and kept commenting on it; later even posting her "learning experience" on facebook.

I flashed back two years to a Vacation Bible School program I had directed. During the week we had arranged for a milk cow to be the evening's demonstration. One of the local vets brought a Holstein to show the kids where milk comes from. I was shocked to see how many kids were surprised and a little disturbed by the location of the milk spigots. A couple of kids dared to touch the teats, but most watched curiously with their hands shoved deep in their pockets.

They were fascinated when the vet took out a milking machine and began explaining how it makes milking more efficient. She gave some of the "bravest" kids a chance to test out the suction to show that it really wasn't going to hurt the cow. Afterward, to demonstrate how much milk a cow can give, the vet asked if anyone would like to come pick up the canister. A few volunteers tried unsuccessfully until one little girl shouted "Why is the can so warm?"

The explanation brought a series of "gross," "eeeeew," "that is so disgusting," and "I'm never drinking milk again!" from all over the group. I was amazed. I still thought of this as a rural farming community, yet most of these kids didn't realize that milk came from the warm udder of a cow.

A big bump jolted me back into the present. I had given up the driver's seat to my friend's daughter, and she was (for the most part) enjoying her first tractor-driving experience.

Tractors don't steer quite like compact cars, and she was working hard to keep the tractor pointed straight down the row. The baler wasn't real pleased with the uneven feed of straw and the direction arrows kept flashing red. Right, left, right, then left again. "Ahhh," she moaned, "if the stupid computer wasn't so bipolar I could drive better!" I snorted a laugh again—I knew balers were temperamental...but I'd never realized they could have real clinical disorders...I guess it was a "learning experience" for all of us today.

12 things I learned at the Farm Fair

*I*t's December! That means Christmas plays, lambing out sheep...and pesticide recertification classes. I headed off for a couple of days at the Farm Fair. It was a couple of days filled with great potato products, lots of interesting new ag products, a few familiar faces, and lots and lots of meetings. While there though, I did learn a few things:

1. I could never be one of the lecturers: I've never described bugs as "beautiful," and I've never looked at them long enough to change my mind. I see a bug, I start spraying or smashing...if I reach for anything it's a fly swatter...not a camera and a notebook.

2. There are many different ways to sleep with your eyes open. And most of them are even drool-free!

3. The delicious potatoes they feed you in the lobby can add to your sleepiness.

4. Time moves slower in front of the podium than behind it.

5. Weeds? No worries—just add flags and call it research!

6. Lawyers will soon be used instead of mice for future

research. There are more of them, people have more compassion for mice, and you can get lawyers to do things mice won't.

7. Low-lit auditoriums are conducive to mid-afternoon naps. But not to worry—the free hats the vendors give you help hide sleeping eyes.

8. Don't worry about writing down the names of the chemicals used in test studies. They're probably not labeled for your crops or legal in your state.

9. The more you look for bugs, the more likely you are to find them.

10. My idea of "cool" isn't biological controls.

11. The scary diseases talked about in the meetings are covered by the insurance companies in the booths outside. Hmmmm.......

12. People actually read what I write! I was delighted to meet several of my loyal readers. Thank you!

Shopping

Whoever said money can't buy happiness...
never shopped at a farm auction.

Shopping guidelines for men

Christmas, Valentines, birthdays and anniversaries can be headache inducers for women who have men on their shopping lists...which is just about all of us. It doesn't matter if it is your father, uncle, grandpa, brother or husband... adult men are difficult to shop for. If they don't have it, they probably don't want it—unless it's too expensive, in which case you are still out of luck.

For Christmas this year, my brother-in-law emailed everyone a "do not wish for" list:

1. Gloves, I'm still working on the pack my dad bought me 3 years ago.

2. Things I have to wear, unless it says KTM on it.

3. Cookbooks. I still use the directions on the back of the box.

4. Underwear, I'm pleased with how mine have been holding up this year.

5. A star registered in my name

6. Literature, my ADHD won't allow me to read any article more than a page.

7. Anything that could possibly be used in the kitchen.

8. Things made out of wool.

(I had to stifle the urge to make him a pair of wool underwear with KTM printed across them!) And while his email may (or may not have) helped getting him a gift, it did get me thinking about how to shop for men, and I came up with some guidelines:

Rule 1: When in doubt, buy him a cordless drill. It doesn't matter if he already has one. They are like man shoes…he can never have too many.

Rule 2: Buy him anything with the word torque in it. Men love torque. No one knows why.

Rule 3: Tickets to a farm expo is a smart gift. Tickets to the opera are not. Everyone knows why.

Rule 4: Buy him something for his vehicle. Men love gifts for their cars, trucks and/or motorcycles…even if they are not in running condition.

Rule 5: Do not buy men socks. Do not buy men ties. And never buy men bathrobes. I was told that if men were supposed to wear bathrobes, Jockey shorts would have never been invented.

Rule 6: Do not buy them industrial-sized cans of deodorant. I was told they don't stink—they are earthy.

Rule 7: Never buy a man anything that says "some assembly required" on the box. He will always have parts left over, and it will ruin his day.

Rule 8: Good places to shop for men include Napa, Sears, Home Depot, Harbor Freight, John Deere, and the Polaris or Yamaha dealership.

Rule 9: Men enjoy danger. Get him a monster barbecue with a 100-pound propane tank. Tell him the gas line leaks. Oh the thrill! The challenge! And I'll bet you'll get supper out of the deal!

Rule 10: Buy a ladder. It's hard to beat a really good aluminum extension ladder. One word of caution though: it must not be a step ladder.

And Rule 11: Men love chainsaws. They'll spend hours carving up anything around them. Never, ever, buy a man a chainsaw.

Impulse buys

Recently, an unnamed radio personality was raving about the problems of America. He ranted about global warming, and terrorism, but one worse he likened to the devastation of holy wars—shopping. He claimed that impulse buying was going to the end of our planet and if everyone in the world shopped like American women we would have to create anther entire world for storage.

While I don't think shopping should be compared to holy wars, it did get me thinking. Typically when people think of shopping, they do seem to make connections to the gentler sex. Consensus seems to say that women enjoy shopping more than men—and because of this enjoyment, do it more often.

And that may be true. Maybe. But when it comes to impulse buying, I will have to say I think it hits the genders pretty equally.

Just this year, a dear professor of mine decided he would like to plant a few strawberry plants in his garden—to which his wife was very agreeable. I can only imagine the thoughts she might have had when she discovered that a "few strawberry plants" actually consisted of one thousand, three hundred and seventy-five strawberry plants!

A few months ago, I waved my husband off to an evening air brakes class. I expected him to return in 4-5 hours with an air brake certification card and less fuel in the tank. 5 hours later he returned cardless, and there was less fuel in the tank...but it was a new tank attached to a new Chevy pickup.

Remind me again why it is women who are labeled impulse buyers?

eBay-cation

7 recently embarked on an exiting eBay-cation. For those of you not quite familiar with this term…it is a trip across the United States for the sole purpose of obtaining items your dad/brother/husband purchased on eBay—with a 14-month-old.

Our adventure started early on a Wednesday morning. We had to wake baby to make it to our 7 a.m. flight (he doesn't like to rise and shine before 8:30 or 9). I was very apprehensive about the flight. We weren't scheduled to land in Tampa, Florida, until midnight—that's a very long time to be confined with a baby—especially one who was awakened early! I breathed a sigh of relief as we finally touched down—my husband had fussed more than the baby.

Now, an eBay-cation should not be confused with a family vacation. The purpose of a vacation is to see new sights and relax. The purpose of an eBay-cation is to bring home vehicles/equipment in as few days as possible. Seeing new sights may occur—relaxing will not—as hurdles are expected side effects of the trip. Our first hurdle was encountered upon landing. We arrived at 12:15 a.m. and discovered the hotel shuttles only run until midnight. Other hurdles included bad bearings, wiring problems, and finding diesel at gas stations in the South.

We picked up the first pickup in Clearwater, Florida, and began our 3,000-mile journey back home. We drove past many interesting tourist attractions and bizarre local sights—many times wanting to stop and explore—but those are things you do on a vacation—not eBay-cation. So we kept driving.

We picked up a cultivator and fertilizer tanks in Lexington, Illinois, and then a second pickup in Des Moines, Iowa. The plan was to haul the second pickup so I wouldn't have to drive alone with the baby. But, as luck would have it, U-haul doesn't make a long enough trailer. So baby and I found ourselves driving the remaining 2/3 of the journey alone. Lucky for me, baby was bitten by the travel bug early (14 states in 14 months) and seemed to enjoy the long road trip.

We weren't done 'eBuying' though. We were about to enter Nebraska, when my dad called and wanted us to look at a corn planter in Kearney. We stopped; the price was good, the only problem seemed to be how to haul it home. U-haul's trailers still weren't long enough...so when you can't rent...eBuy.

One week later we pulled into our driveway with a one-ton flatbed Duramax loaded up with saddle tanks and a cultivator, another Duramax pulling a flatbed trailer with a 6-row corn planter—and a camera full of pictures from rest areas across 9 states!

I believe every trip has at least one learning experience—so what was ours? Ebay-cations and Interstates are the fastest way to travel cross country while seeing absolutely nothing!

Breakdowns & Accidents

Engine Repair Price List

Ping- Ping -Ping..............$35
Plunk - Ping-Plunk..........$55
Clunk-Ping-Clunk.......$125
Thud-Klunk-Thud......$200
Clang- Thud- Klank.. $325

I'm a Chevy girl

I'm a Chevy girl—and probably always will be. And if asked why, I can come up with at least 10 reasons off the top of my head. But when it really comes down to it, it's just apples and oranges. Some people prefer apples, others oranges. Does it really matter? But to some people it apparently does.

I'm sure you've seen the bumper stickers: "I'd rather push a Ford than drive a Chevy," and vice versa. While I'm certainly a Chevy girl, and if buying a new vehicle, you'll not see me at the Ford dealership, I'm not too sure about pushing anything: Fords, Chevys, Dodges, lawnmowers....

The people displaying those bumper stickers must either be related to the Hulk or perhaps they've never been stranded on a back road, in 90-degree weather, with little-to-no-hope of spotting a passing car.

Just a few weeks ago, I was driving out of town—just me and my dog, Iliad—when the pickup decided to take a break. I was several miles from any house, on a little gravel road, without my cellphone, while the thermometer in the cab illuminated three blue digits.

With sweat running down my face, I rubbed the steering wheel, telling it what a nice pickup it was; I wiped down the dash and told it how much better the gauges looked with the windows rolled up and the air conditioner blowing in my face. 15 minutes of platitudes and the pickup still wouldn't start. Finally I rolled up the windows, pocketed the keys, and told Illi it was time to walk. She looked at me with sweat dripping off her tongue and gave me a look I'm glad wasn't translated.

We walked a couple of miles, before getting a ride with a guy in a swather. Boy I'm glad farmers make hay when the sun shines. Later that evening, after getting the pickup running again, I saw one of those bumper stickers reading: "I'd rather push a Chevy than drive a Ford." I looked at the driver as I passed, a white T-shirt, khaki pants, and I imagined him to have well-manicured nails, and I just shook my head.

I wonder if they'd change their mind if they were ever stranded somewhere and had to walk. Nope, I may like Chevys, but when it comes to pushing—I'd rather drive an old beat up Ford Ranger, than push a late model Chevy Duramax.

Murphy's law invades tractor cab

Some days are best enjoyed in bed. The day had started beautiful. I had woke soon enough to shut off my alarm clock before it jarred me into another day.

Bright rays shone through the curtains onto an empty laundry hamper (life doesn't get much better than clean laundry!), and I could smell hash browns sizzling from the kitchen. I should have taken a deep breath and gone back to bed—instead, I found myself sitting amongst thousands of glass shards.

It was my own fault, I had thought the unthinkable. I was raking; two fields down and only the outside rounds of the third one left. As I drove down the rows I began thinking of how productive the day had been: the dishes washed, the litter box cleaned, boy, things were going well today!

I reached the end of the row and lifted up the rake to make a cleaner turn. One hand was on the rake control while the other was flat-handing the steering wheel. I am looking over my shoulder to avoid catching the fence when I see the rake drop like it fell in a deep hole.

Suddenly with the instant slow motion of a strobe light, the rake control box starts moving. I notice the rake has stopped following the tractor.

With painful slowness I grab for the throttle and jam my flip flops onto the pedals. My dog slaps into the windshield at the same instant that the rake control box slips out of its clasp and takes the shortest distance back to the rake— right through the back window. The hoses hooked to the tractor had break-away clips that didn't break and the hoses had gone taut and finally snapped like writhing snakes hissing as they flung hydraulic oil through the air.

So there I sat in a chair full of broken glass. My only company a frightened dog and a laughing Murphy, highlighting a list of laws I had disregarded.

But I learned my two valuable lessons. First, don't ever even think the day is going well....for it soon won't be. And most important, if you awake to warm sun rays on your face and the smell of your favorite meal wafting across your nose—don't wait for Murphy to ruin you day. Take life into your own hands—pick up the phone, call your mother-in-law and ruin it yourself.

They met by accident...

*T*he light was red. A man on a motorcycle slowed to a stop, enjoying the warm sun while the cool breeze brushed across his cheeks. Suddenly the sound of tires squealing pierced the idyllic scene. The motorcyclist stiffened, bracing against the handlebars a split second before he was rear ended. His bike slid forward and into the car ahead of him. The bike was totaled, but, thankfully, the man himself was not injured.

The offending car's bumper grated against metal as it backed away from what minutes before was a pleasant bike ride. Rolling down the window, the woman driver hollered out that she was just going to drive around the corner and get out of traffic. The motorcyclist nodded, as he began to drag the twisted vestiges of his motorcycle off the road. Beads of sweat were beginning to trail down his forehead as he dragged the last piece of his motorcycle off the road. Minutes later, he stepped back to survey the damage—that's when he noticed two very important things missing—the woman driver and her car.

The police soon arrived and began questioning the motorcyclist as to the identity of the woman; he shrugged. He'd only met her by accident. "What about the car?" He didn't know, he'd gotten little more than a cursory glance before she'd driven off. "Is there anything else that might identify her?" the cop asked. But the motorcyclist wasn't listening.

He'd just noticed something smashed between the seat and the tail light. He reached down, and wedged in the back of his bike was a little souvenir from his wreck—the front license plate from the woman's car! The motorcyclist—my uncle—chuckled as he remembered how surprised he was to find that little memento.

His accident taught me 2 things: 1. Be sure your sins will find you out. And 2: It takes 8,460 bolts to assemble an automobile, one nut to scatter it all over the road, and a lone license plate to point the blame!!

Computer commitment calamity

*S*aying I Do to a computer is not a 2-way relationship. Instead it is a long list of "I Do's" that you must promise to complete for as long as the computer chooses to live: I Do promise to keep you backed up. I Do promise to get all your new updates. I Do promise to protect you from virus/malware/spy ware.

And in return the computer promises no fidelity, no loyalty and certainly no love or respect.

Last month during my morning routine of checking in with facebook friends, my laptop decided it needed some space—permanently. The screen went blue and started humming.

At nearly the precise moment that my computer was locking up, my brain opened a file entitled: Last Time You Backed Up Your Files. Funny how 10 minutes before I wouldn't have had a clue the last time I backed up my files...or what files I even had on the computer...but that blank screen seemed to be like a hotshot to my brain, and I began to recall all kinds of irreplaceable pictures and data stored behind that infidel piece of plastic. A blue screen staring at me, taunting me with white letters flashing "System Failure" seemed akin to, "I think we should see other people."

So I did what anyone with a broken computer does...I called a friend for consolation. The separation was difficult and I was unsure how to fill the empty desk the computer had left behind. This hiatus lasted 3 weeks, and I felt a twinge every time I looked over and saw his desk get covered in papers, files and grease zircs. I supposed I should have thrown out the power cord and all his personal effects, but I couldn't completely extinguish the hope that he would realize how good he had it here and come back.

Finally my computer came home, with most of his files restored. I was delighted! And I promised him I'd back up his hard drive monthly, maybe weekly...possibly even daily.

I got my external hard drive out and set up, ready to transfer over the files that I'd been lucky to get back. That's when the goats got out, then the neighbor dog came visiting, and the tire exploded on the tractor. I thought about transferring all that recovered data that night...but...and then...and after that....

Four days later, I was back on facebook, when the screen went black. I suddenly realized just how high-maintenance this relationship really was. I had committed to it with a "til death do us part" attitude, whereas he was really more of a boyfriend. The fickle kind that you don't dare leave your favorite CD in his vehicle because you may never see either of them again. I guess when it comes to technology monogamy is overrated....

My physics lesson...

I recently took a crash course in applied physics; more specifically Newton's laws of motion. His first law states that if an object experiences no net force then its velocity is constant. I was moving through harvest season at a constant speed and direction—until a few weeks ago. It was one of those weeks where everything went exceptionally well. I received free tickets to the rodeo, the PBR, a box of apples, a delicious homemade apple pie, we had no significant machinery breakdowns, I got to spend a day at the river, and a good-looking stranger brought me a bouquet of roses to the farmers market. It was a great week.

Which took me to Newton's second law of motion. The acceleration of a body is parallel and directly proportional to the net force acting on the body. Thus far the force was good, which kept my week propelling in an amazing direction.

Unfortunately however, Newton's third law states that for every action there is an equal and opposite reaction. We kicked off the next week by roading the swather home; my husband misjudged the width of the header and wedged it securely between the guardrails of a little bridge.

Then there was the premature retirement party of our

semi-truck, we celebrated by towing it off the highway. A working semi was a necessity, so at 3 a.m. I packed up my sleeping toddler and sent my husband off to Utah in search of another semi-truck.

We got back from the airport around 6, and I had just snuggled back into bed, when my phone rang. A breathless voice asked, "Did you know one of your calves is nearly dead?" I grabbed yesterday's clothes and headed out for the week's dramatic climax. With the help of a neighbor, the calf was tubed and given some much-needed antibiotics. I was still in the pasture, when someone came to pick up their melon order, and of course, it was wrong. The melon fiasco was just about completed when a friend called looking for an electric buffer.

With our house being packed up, I doubted my ability to find it, but thought there might be a chance it was in our basement. I bounded down the stairs—right into several inches of water.

The toilet had broken and was overflowing, and the septic had plugged; and between the two, my entire basement was under water. Books, college papers, boxes of memoirs—all those things that a basement seems to collect—were wet, soggy and most of them ruined.

That's when I received my greatest physics lesson of all. Physics, in a broad sense, is understanding how the universe works.

I discovered that when your week is bad, your house floods and makes a huge stinky mess, that a true friend doesn't just sympathize….a true friend shows up wearing rubber boots, gloves, mask, and armed with loads of cleaning supplies (or tubing supplies and antibiotics) and will "work" to put your "universe" back together.

What can you buy with $670?

$670 bought us adventure filled with emergency vehicles, smoke and a lot of adrenaline. The day dawned bright and warm and our friends decided to take out their new "steal of a boat." We packed a picnic lunch, grabbed life jackets for all and headed out to the river. Food, friends, and fabulous weather—we were preparing to make some good memories—we just didn't realize how memorable they were going to be!

We dropped the boat in the water and piled in at the docks, and waited...and waited...and waited. Seemed like their "steal" had a few attitude issues. She finally started, but that stubborn teenager of a boat, coughed and sputtered and growled all the way out past the breakwater. My husband was sitting on the bench covering the engine compartment when she started making some clunking noises, and then started spewing a bit of smoke.

Thinking it was probably just old fuel, our friends kept on heading out toward the river's center. The smoke, however, kept getting worse. Suddenly I noticed it was coming out the cupholders where I was sitting. I jumped up, grabbed my son and practically knocked my friends over to get to the bow of the boat, as far away from the engine as I could get.

By now, the smoke had engulfed the back of the boat, and the fire extinguisher on board didn't work. Meanwhile I stood on the bow, alternating between waving for help and taking pictures—so in case the boat exploded and we all died, someone would have evidence as to what happened.

I don't know how many minutes elapsed until this point— it was probably something like 20—but it seemed like the start of a "three-hour tour." Another boat came with a fire extinguisher and the smoke finally subsided. A second boat from shore had seen the commotion and had come to see if all was okay, they ended up towing us back to the dock— where we were met by a sheriff, a wildfire vehicle, another cop car, and a fire truck.

$670 can buy you smoke, excitement, and heart-pumping, adrenaline-throbbing adventure; $670 cannot buy you smooth sailing.

Anchors & super powers

I discovered I have super powers—well at least one power—eye power. Let me start at the beginning. Recently, my sister and I were enjoying the cool breeze of the Columbia River from my brother's new boat. As the day progressed, so did the wind; which led us to a shallow inlet, where we intended to drop anchor and play water Frisbee. At the last minute we decided to take my boat along too.

My brother found a nice location that wasn't more than four feet deep, and my sister tossed the anchor over the front. The rope whipped through the boat and over the seats seconds before it followed the anchor to the bottom of the muddy river. We all stood in stunned silence for a second, before my brother's friend jumped in to attempt a rescue. It was a nice, but futile gesture, and my brother mourned the loss of his anchor and "new, expensive rope," while we tossed in our (connected) anchor and they tied up to us.

Some of us played in the water, some tanned, and my little boy shot us all with water guns, but we finally decided to call it a day—that's when we found the anchor rope. His prop had devoured the rope, but the anchor was still nowhere to be seen.

The next day the water was worse. Almost too rough for

the boat. So we ended up back in the same area with goggles and a super-magnet to find the lost anchor. Hours passed, but to my brother's disappointment (and merciless teasing of my sister about "anchor's away" instead of "anchor's aweigh"), the anchor remained lost.

The water remained rough all day; we kept making little runs out hoping it would smooth out, but it never did. It finally calmed down enough we got the tubes out, and I took a short run out with two other girls. The details are fuzzy, but the water was rougher than we'd anticipated, and we crashed hard.

My brother always says "no pain, no glory," but I was having a hard time remembering that laying in the emergency room getting a CT scan. I could barely speak, didn't know my birthdate, and standing took effort. I had bruised my brain.

They finally let me go home; I went straight to bed, and slept for nearly three full days, and cat-napped the rest of the week. Five days later, the fog started to clear, and that's when I noticed my super power.

Dirty dishes were piled in the sink, plates with half eaten sandwiches covered the coffee table, toys were everywhere but their box, laundry was piled up, four empty toilet paper rolls on the floor, one on holder and the full roll propped up on the towel rack. And I was the only person who seemed to see it! So, I reasoned, I must have super eye powers.

Too bad I didn't realize that earlier, I might have found the lost anchor—along with the mysterious lever that allows new rolls of toilet paper to be put onto the holder.

Living the Life of Riley

I enjoy listening to radio dramas, and one of my favorites has always been the Life of Riley. The situations he gets himself into and the rather dead remarks by Digger O'Dell. Chester A. Riley once said, "Some guys have an off day…I have an off life." That was my motto last week when a rather awful accident turned funny with our twisted Digger O'Dell humor.

My phone buzzed in my pocket; I ignored it as I continued to dig lima bean vines out of my swather header. I jammed a stalk under my nail and groaned. I looked across the field, my husband was still stopped—his baler probably plugged as full of mud and lima beans as my swather was. We had been fighting this field all day. I grabbed at another wad of dirt and vines, it came loose suddenly and I fell, gashing my back on the header. I stood up and decided to take a break and check my messages. I pulled out my phone and saw a picture of my dad's "off-life day." Driving through the field, the entire back axle suddenly decided to come off the swather.

I could almost hear Digger O'Dell's voice coming out of the axles saying "Cheerio…I'd better be shoveling off…"

And suddenly, the day seemed brighter. Riley's life was one mishap after another, and they always found time to laugh, why shouldn't we? And that began the playful banter of texts.

•Next time you say "sit" make sure the swather knows you are talking to the dog riding passenger!

•It looks like it was a real "let down."

•Talk about the bottom falling out of your world.

•I thought things were looking up...then I realized it was just me.

•Sitting down on the job again...?

•I knew airplanes could be tail draggers, but swathers?

•I think it's okay, it just needs a little "pick me up."

•Maybe you should go Hesston—they never let you down.

•It's not a very upstanding piece of machinery...it's more of a lowlife.

•You know life has its ups and downs...I guess swathers do too.

•Actually, I think the swather had a crush on the alfalfa.

•You know this is going in a column right? Something entitled "dog commands for swathers." It has already mastered "sit," "stay," and "play dead." Now I'm just waiting for it to roll over.

I can almost hear Riley exclaim, "What a revoltin' development this is." Welcome to the Life of Riley!

Farm Girls

A farm girl remembers the first car she bought,
the first boy she kissed,
and the first tractor she drove.

Tractors, sweat, & Speedos

*W*ithout getting into the battle of the sexes, I must say that I think there are quite a few things that make life easier on men. They don't have to shave below their neck. The same hairstyle lasts for years—sometimes decades.

Buying flowers for your significant other will fix everything. Men don't retain water—and if they do—it's in a canteen. Wrinkles add character and white hair distinguishes. Men also have freedom of choice about growing a mustache.

The playing field really becomes imbalanced when farming. The sun will be blaring down at 100 degrees on two people—one man, one woman. Soon one back will be shirtless taking advantage of the slight breeze—you can be sure that it will rarely be the female.

Hours later, after having relocated 25 tons of hay, both people will be sticky. By our social conventions men are allowed—even expected to sweat heavily, while women are only allowed to dew, or perhaps perspire under the right circumstances. And at the end of the day, dirt under the man's nails will be acceptable.

But the real inequalities show up in an empty field with a full bladder. The man and woman are each in a tractor. The man's tractor will make occasional stops so he can "check the tires." The woman, after looking unsuccessfully for a shrub or tree, will drive with one leg tucked under her and then the other, until the field is finished and she hobbles painfully to the pickup.

I'm not complaining about being a woman—after all we got off the Titanic first, we don't look like a frog in a blender when dancing, and no fashion faux pas we ever make could rival the Speedo. We can stop and ask for directions before driving the wrong way through 5 states, and we can go to a movie with a friend without needing an empty chair between us—but there are some definite advantages to being a male farmer.

It is easier for men to recall seeding rates due to their excessive practice memorizing sports scores, a full bladder in a field without bushes is never a problem, and the paramount inequality? Men can hide dirty hair by wearing a dirty hat.

Personality disorder? Of course not!

*P*eople always say you are what you eat and that you can tell a lot about someone by looking at their heroes. I knew that made me a little light and fluffy, a few hulls lingering long after the butter had dissolved, and some left-over old maids to round out my popcorn personality.

I was okay with that. Popcorn is a feel-good food, so I assumed, that for all my flaws, I still made people feel good. So the "you are what you eat" philosophy never bothered me.

And my heroes were all great (after all, that's why they were my heroes!) So I never worried about their effects on me either...that is, until I got a phone call from my sister.

She is in med school and is currently working in a psych hospital. During a recent class her instructor was lecturing on personality disorders, "...and this disorder is best modeled by Scarlet O'Hara...."

My sister could barely concentrate on the rest of the class. She and I had grown up idolizing the beautiful, determined Scarlet O'Hara. We'd watch with admiration at her collection of beaus, and then after the war arrived her determination to survive. Her creativity, when designing her beautiful gown out of the draperies would make us smile, and even though we shed tears when Rhett left, it was okay—after all, she still had Tara. And now to hear that this professor thought she had a personality disorder? Something about emotional detachment or some such nonsense!

But it made me pause as I thought about my other favorite characters: Data (the emotionless android), Captain Kirk (the handsome officer would kiss his female captor while he stole her keys, then knock her unconscious as he escaped) and of course Lisa Douglas (the gorgeous blond wife of the lawyer-turned-farmer on Green Acres).

So what does that say about me? Am I a relationship-challenged, emotionless player who thinks chickens lay square eggs and my cow will give me a saucer of milk at a time?

I think it's about time someone debunks that philosophy...I think you should be able to tell more about a person by what kind of dog they have!

It's a size thing

I have always preferred hanging out with the guys: if I had to choose between grease-monkeying in the shop with the guys, or doing my nails with the girls... well, who says red nails are more attractive than greasy ones?

But as much as I enjoy the male companionship, I don't always get the point of their activities. Their unwritten code seems to be: "my dad's bigger than your dad...my dog's faster than your dog...my mom's cooler than your mom...my tractor's stronger than your tractor...."

My sister and I sat at the bottom of a very large sand dune. We were watching the guys drive up and down it. They would stop at the base, hit the throttle and see which one could make it the farthest up the hill before turning back.

My sister and I couldn't figure out the fun of it. There was no jumping, no exceptional skill needed to perform the task...it seemed to us simply a matter of whose machine was more powerful. When they finally all had reached the top, they hung the front tires of their four-wheelers over the edge of the sand, and seemed to be preening.

We were almost surprised they didn't find a flag to plant at the top—after all, their body language seemed to scream "We came, we saw, we climbed!!"

While watching them strut their stuff, we decoded the original lyrics to an old folk song—we think it should have been written like this:

"The man went over the mountain...the man went over the mountain. The man went over the mountain...to prove he could beat the mountain. (or the other men)." I guess the person that said size doesn't matter must have been a woman...either that or a man with a very small four-wheeler!

Highway melon thief

My speedometer read 65 mph; my fuel gauge nearly empty; my rearview mirror showed the 40-something man stretched out between the passenger window of his white van and the bin of melons on my trailer. I've always considered my watermelon runs between Hermiston and Portland "adventures," but the one that took the cake happened 6 years ago.

The day dawned bright and sunny—and too perfect to stay that way. Cruising down the highway with a bit of tailwind and George Jones on the radio, life was good. Then I drove through Mosier.

A white van filled with middle-aged men pulled up beside me, and started leering and making obscene gestures. I turned up the radio and attempted to ignore them. The van matched my speed and drove parallel to my driver window for a good 5 minutes. When they didn't succeed in drawing my attention, they pulled a few feet ahead and began climbing out the window, making lewd motions

Soon the van began lagging behind, then pulling ahead, never getting more than a car length away from me. It wasn't long before they had crossed the center line and began edging into my lane. My palms were sweaty. Crazy old men weren't covered in my driver's manual. After 15+ minutes of this, the van pulled alongside my trailer and the passenger began to climb out the window. With shaking hands I dialed 911.

I told the officer a man was attempting to climb onto my trailer while driving down the freeway at 65 mph. "Someone's holding his ankles...he's got a melon now...oh he dropped it...he's trying for another one... what do I do?"

"Ma'am, how old are you?"

"What difference does that make?" I asked. Watching as the man stretched out his window farther and farther, finally lunging to catch the bin on my trailer. It looked like a stunt out of Hollywood. He was right in front of my axles. If he slipped and fell, I would most likely run over him...would I be liable? I expressed my concern to the police officer. Who politely told me 911 was for real emergencies and promptly disconnected.

After dropping two melons, the man finally succeeded in stealing the third. With much whooping and hollering the man pulled his prize into the van and sped away. That alone could have been my adventure—but little did I know—my melon run was just beginning.

My fingers clenched white on the steering wheel. The white van carrying the middle-aged melon thieves pulled over in front of me and slowed down. My shaking foot backed off the throttle—the last thing I wanted to do was pass them and start this fiasco over again.

As my speedometer dial slowed, the van finally started to pull away from me. I breathed a sigh of relief— prematurely.

They were taking my exit—the one I needed for fuel. My wallet had a driver's license, a handful of library cards for around the state, a scuba certification card, and a couple coins from Thailand and a Pacific Pride card. I didn't have much choice as to where to get fuel—and they took the exit and pulled into the convenience store—right next to the Pacific Pride.

Alone, scared, cellphone dead, and down 3 melons already, there was no way I was going to stop—no matter how low my fuel gauge was. I gave one last glance at the crazy men, now getting out of the van, and the red, orange and yellow Pacific Pride sign, and began praying I had enough fumes to coax me to the next Pacific Pride.

The pickup was sputtering as I took the 181st Street exit. I pulled into the turn lane of the 5-lane road. The light turned red just as I reached the intersection. I slowed to a stop, the first vehicle at the light.

The Pacific Pride was just ¼ mile down the road. The light was taking forever to turn green. And as my luck would have it that day, just as the light changed—the pickup took its last wheezing gulp of diesel.

The line of cars behind me started honking. I put my flashers on. A red car squealed around me as the driver flipped me off. He was the first in a long line of birds. With no one knowing where I was or the predicament I was in—it was up to me to get out—somehow. I left the pickup and trailer load of melons, and walked across the street to a Shell station. As I walked in the door, one of the employees was commenting on the commotion in the intersection as angry drivers honked and shouted insults.

Upon discovering that I was the driver, she took pity on me and bought me a small gas can. A patron there offered to buy the fuel for it. I offered melons in return but the lady just told me to pay her back on my next trip through. Several people in the store, overhearing my dilemma offered to pitch in to buy me a couple gallons of fuel.

Another patron, on his way to his daughter's birthday party, followed me back to the pickup to make sure I'd be okay. That was when I learned the hard way just what a bad idea it is to let a diesel run out of fuel.

25 minutes later, we're still sitting there—trying to ignore the honking. We bled the lines, and disconnected the battery—all with a screwdriver and a pocket knife—and finally through the help of several strangers, I was back en route to deliver my melons.

Squeaky wheels & noisy ducks

I did it again. Me and my big mouth. They say the squeaky wheel gets greased, but I'm starting to believe more in the Japanese proverb that the noisy duck gets shot. But let me start at the beginning. We have an old John Deere riding lawn mower that has more quirks than one personality should be allowed.

Starting it is not accomplished by a mere turn of the key—that would be too easy. Instead, one must remove the hood, and put the battery on the charger. While the battery is charging, the front tire must be aired up. It currently holds 6 rubber plugs, 2 bottles of tire sealant, and a determination to be flat. Once the tire is taken care of, it is time to start the engine. One must take a plastic handled screw driver and spark across the starter solenoid. Once it starts, the hood needs replaced, and you are almost ready to go. Just remember not to use the brake. The cable is broke somewhere inside, and if the pedal is pushed, the brakes lock up—and it's a job to release them.

These are the steps I've taken each time I've mowed the lawn for the past 7 years. Depending on the attitude of the lawn mower, this process can take up to 45 minutes before it even sees grass. Last year I decided something had to be done. I decided to let the lawn grow without cutting it, and perhaps my husband would take the hint and fix the mower—without any prompting.

Soon we began losing small items in the grass: balls, glasses, and keys. When my husband joked about harvesting a few bales of grass hay off our yard, I thought something would finally be done...but bringing in the swather wasn't exactly what I had in mind.

This spring I implemented Plan B: the squeaky wheel method. Squeaky wheels squeak, right? So squeak I did. Days before I was to mow the lawn I would go into great detail about how difficult it was to start it, how frustrating it was to always fix the flat, and how hard it was to mow around obstacles without using the brakes. And then I shot myself in the foot. "Even my old electric push mower in college started easier than this old beast."

Fast forward to May Day. While everyone else was getting showered in pretty blossoms, my shower was in lawn clippings from my new push mower. My husband was glowing with satisfaction, and looked a little puzzled at my thinly veiled disgust.

"You said a push lawn mower would work better, so I thought I'd surprise you with one!" And surprise me he did. 5 hours of walking behind a mower is a lot of time to ponder that squeaky wheel method, and I must tell you I'm feeling more like the noisy duck that got shot. And judging from the blisters on my feet, I'd say my mouth shot got off a good round, right into my feet.

Sinus monsters
& circus performers

Laugh and the world laughs with you...
Snore, and you sleep alone...

*M*y husband was snoring like a seal, and I was struggling with my decision to kick him or throw fish. I nudged him. He snorted, then stopped. The silence that ensued was divine. I nestled down into my covers and had just reached the point of dreams when the hhhoooyaaabbbahoonkrababa-bashoooo started again. It was like listening to Fred Flintstone with a sinus infection. I nudged harder this time. Again the snoring would stop just long enough for me to drift off. This cycled repeatedly. Finally I shook him awake. "Roll over, you're snoring so loud you're chasing the monsters in my dreams," I grumbled.

I knew he had had a long day with a lot of field work and equipment breakdowns, and he was fighting off a head cold, but my sympathy seemed to dissipate each time his uvula flapped against his throat. I finally turned on an audio book, put a pillow over his head, and fell asleep to dream about cows who snorted like they were in their final death throes.

The next day I was still grumbling about his snoring, and

we got into a "who snores louder" discussion. I snore. I admit it, but not always, and never louder than him. He disagreed. My proof? He falls asleep first.

The days passed, our discussion however, didn't.

Then one afternoon while moving equipment out to the field, my husband hands me his phone. "Listen to this," he says. I held it up to my ear. I didn't hear anything but static. "Listen close," he smirks.

I try, but all I hear is this faint static that gets louder and then quieter, then louder again. "Don't you recognize it?" he is gleaming from ear to ear.

Suddenly it dawns on me. "You were snoring so loud last night!!" he chortled, "that I just had to record you!!"

I couldn't believe my ears. "You recorded me?" I ask in disbelief. My disbelief increased as he played the tape for friends and neighbors over the next few days. Our argument over who snores the loudest still hasn't been resolved—but it did make my earlier struggle a little easier. Next time his snoring encroaches on my dreams I have a whole collection of balls and fish for his enjoyment. He wants to snore like a seal—I'm gonna make him a star circus performer.

Move over Al Anon

Sewage spots peppered our shirts faster than the rain could wash it off. Dark streaks smeared across our palms where the glop had stained into our gloves. My husband "doesn't do gross," so as soon as we pulled that Rent-A-Snake out of her car, he decided we needed a girls weekend. It wasn't long before my friend was shoulder deep in...um... organic cuticle softener—a most natural manicure experience. My only complaint was the threat of death if I took any pictures to remember our girl time. A few hours, a torn glove, a sprained finger and two showers later, we were feeling pretty pleased with ourselves. And I was thankful for the rain that caused a break in farming and had allowed the weekend to happen.

After the snake had been returned, and all sign of "gross" had disappeared (minus the bandage around my friend's finger), my husband returned to help pack bags and head for home. His weekend had consisted in a little hiking around Mt. Rainier, and a visit to relatives—which gave us fodder for conversation on the way home. They were planning a trip to Vegas for their birthdays. Vegas, while full of shows and entertainment, never really held much attraction for me (with the exception of the Star Trek Experience).

As the windshield wipers swished across the dash, I thought of all the first-cutting hay turning black around the Valley. We gambled enough without Vegas. Not just penny slots either…we gambled with large machinery payments, and operating loans. And the closest we get to free house drinks, would be the plugged sprinkler that finally spits out the gopher leg and sprays us in the face. When we have a winning year, we're really excited to try it again…and when we have a losing year, we can hardly wait for the ground to thaw so we can try it again.

It's in our blood, plain and simple. We grow up gambling on the sun, the rain, the temperature, the bugs, and of course the market. And every year it's all or nothing. We can't stop. We're addicted. We live, breathe, pray and play farming. I recently watched my son load his grain trailers using the old metal doorstop on the wall as the grain auger, and then hauling them into the hall to market. He can't help it. It's an addiction that runs in families.

One afternoon while on a father/daughter lunch date, my dad's phone rang like a continuous buzzer. "Farming finds you everywhere," he remarked. Which brought up the Vegas/gambling topic. They have AA and NA; it's too bad they don't have an "A" group to join like most addicts, I chortled.

They do, my dad replied. Every town has one—it might be at the corner market, or the irrigation district—but they meet every morning for a cup of coffee and a little friendly field gossip. I had to smile, we'd always called it the "town council meeting," but "Farmer's Anonymous" is probably just as appropriate. A little support group to help us all keep on keeping on. And if that fails, I already know what it feels like to be up to my armpits....

High heeled logos

*W*hy do so many businesses give away free hats to valued customers? Every time my husband goes to buy fertilizer or sell grain he comes home with several new hats. It's the same with the Farmer's Co-op, the oil company, the tire guy, the seed company—and those are just the ones on the night stand. The stack in the closet reminds me a bit of the garbage that Sarah Silvia Cynthia Stout could not seem to ever take out. "It filled the [closet], it covered the floor; It cracked the windows and blocked the door....The [hats] rolled on down the halls, It raised the roof, it broke the walls. At last the [stack] reached so high, That finally it touched the sky...."

Okay, so maybe his hat collection isn't that bad—it hasn't spread into the hallway, it only fills one closet—one whole closet. Which also wouldn't be so bad except it's the same closet I try to keep my shoe collection in. I may not go for the purses or the lipstick, but my girly weakness is heels—and his hats keep encroaching on my shoe space! At last count, his hats outnumbered my shoes 2 to 1.

And it's not as if he mixes and matches his hats, no. He wears the same hat every day till the bill is tattered, the sweat stains are starting to show on the outside and the advertiser's logo is barely visible. That's when his hat takes a mysterious journey to Sarah Stout's garbage collection. This trip always has to be taken on a moonless night, preferably in the middle of harvest when my husband is rummy from sleep deprivation. I'll sneak it off the night stand, and bury it deep into the kitchen garbage can—dumping the chicken scraps on top to ensure the trip is one-way.

The next morning is an exercise in poker faces. As my husband looks under the bed and behind the couch for his "lost" hat, I look too. I look behind the shower curtain and under the rug. "Hmmmm…no hat here…are you sure you wore it home last night? Maybe it fell off when you were working under the baler last night?" After several minutes of the charade, I usually suggest he just wear another one. Sometimes when he takes a new one out of the closet he looks at me like he knows I played a part in his hat's disappearance. But more often than not, he's too busy mourning the loss of an old friend, to notice my little wave to the rest of his hats. I will eventually play flight attendant to all of them: "Goodbye. Enjoy your trip. Goodbye…"

I bet wives would be much more encouraging about repeat shopping if businesses gave away their logos on high- heeled shoes instead of hats! Then, when my husband comes home from buying seed and says excitedly, "Look what they gave me!" I can share his excitement while I look for an outfit to go with Wilbur Ellis shoes. It would be a win-win.

Surprises & Adventures

If you always do what you've always done,
you'll always be what you've always been.
If you always go where you've always gone,
you'll always be, where you've always been.

Zucchini milkshakes

*W*hy is fruitcake given at Christmas time? Do people actually eat that hard and sweet, gooey and indigestible breaded brick? While jingle bells ring and Old Saint Nick starts his winter exercise program, I watch friends and neighbors bringing over those dreaded fruitcakes, and wonder: "are we supposed to eat them, or use them for extra strength in our snow forts?"

I wonder where fruitcakes originated? I can just imagine a desperate castle-wife back in the day of chivalry and jousting, required to make up a basket of goodies during the yuletide for her husband's ex-betrothed. She sits in the kitchen for hours before striking onto an idea. She starts by taking some almost fermenting fruit, and mixes it into a pretty shaped loaf; she adds lots of sugar to make it slightly palatable, then ties a lovely ribbon around it and calls it fruitcake. She has satisfied her social demands, while still feeling like she bested her rivaling neighbor.

Unfortunately, this affront isn't left in the winter months. Fruitcake is to Christmas, what the dreaded zucchini is to summer. How can seed companies continue to sell zucchini seeds when no one seems to enjoy eating the produce? It isn't as if one plant produces one squash—quite the contrary. One seed seems to produce 5 plants, and each plant produces 5 squash—per day, and each squash has roughly 50 seeds which produce 250 plants, which...you get the picture. Yet more seeds are sold every year.

Coming home from work in the evening makes me nervous as there is often a little brown sack on my doorstep, filled to overflowing with (you guessed it) zucchini. Friends shouldn't give friends zucchini. What am I supposed to do with them? There are only so many ways to disguise zucchini: casseroles, stews, pot pies, milkshakes (okay my siblings nearly killed me for whizzing some squash in with their strawberry milkshake...I wouldn't recommend it).

My parents finished work one day and found the front seat of their pickup covered with 3-foot zucchini clubs. If there's one thing that is worse than zucchini...it's giant zucchini. What are they good for? They're not quite straight enough to use for bowling pins, they not curved enough for horse shoes, and they certainly aren't edible. I guess the only thing left is finding another unlocked vehicle and sharing the wealth.

Maybe zucchini aren't that prolific after all. Maybe, like fruitcake they're just passed on forever. One last word of advice, unless you enjoy thinking up new uses for the fearful zucchini, keep your porch under the sprinkler to prevent that friendly zucchini deliverer, and always lock your vehicle doors.

These boots are made for working...

I've always been a sucker for surprises. So when my husband called me at work and said "Rabbit, (my nickname) I have a surprise for you,"—I was very excited. The hour drive home had me dreaming up all sorts of exotic gifts: an updated, unabridged Webster's dictionary; new charcoal art pencils; or maybe tickets to a Chinese circus.

My husband greeted me at the door with a kiss and a cup of tea. After taking my jacket, he led me into the living room where a large box was setting on the piano bench. All wrapped up in crimson wrapping—it looked promising.

"Open it. Open it." he was urging (he has very little patience when it comes to gifts—whether giving or receiving). Which is just fine by me, as I've been wondering what it could be for over an hour.

As I begin tearing the paper, I am suddenly curious as to the purpose of this gift. It isn't my birthday, Rabbit Day (my own holiday), our anniversary, or any other

occasion I could think of—not that I was complaining...
yet.

The wrapping hid a brown box with the inscription
Muck Boots. Inside the box was my very own pair of
rubber boots, which were "insulated, breathable, neo-
prene, padded soles..." my husband continued with his
sales pitch while I heard nothing but "...so now you can
help me change handline!!!" What love, what companionship, what a way to get free labor.

Recently, I again came home to find a crimson-striped
package on the kitchen table addressed to me. With a
little more apprehension this time, I cautiously began re-
moving the masking tape. As the paper tore I saw the
letters ...OOTS on the edge of the box. Looking up at a
grinning husband, I thought of throwing the box at him.
But maybe he just used the same box? Wrong. This time
he had bought me my very own...(drum roll please)...
work boots. "So now I don't have to get hay or straw
stuck in my sneakers anymore...." All I heard was "so
now you can...."

If I receive any more surprise gifts, I can pretty much
count out that new encyclopedia set I've been wanting—
I think my husband has a foot fetish. Either that or he's
just trying to protect his lucky Rabbit's foot.

Redneck wedding cake

As the groom walked up to the front wearing a camouflage-colored tux, I knew I was in for my first real redneck wedding. I was moving closer to the front to get some good shots of the bride, when a hush fell over the audience, and Billy Idol came booming out of a stereo on the porch: "It's a good day for a…white wedding!"

The bride danced her way to the front while I snapped pictures. When she and the groom linked fingers I began to move to the other side to get better pictures of the bridesmaids.

I heard the officiant begin with the usual: "Welcome, we are all gathered here to witness this marriage between two very wonderful people." The next sentence startled me. "Do you take her to be your lawfully wedded wife?" Boy this couple wasted no time at all. Before I could make it over to photograph the bridesmaids, the ceremony was over and they were walking back down the isle. By my reckoning the whole thing took about 3 minutes!

The newlyweds walked out under an antler covered arch and on to the reception. There beside the tent, people were playing horseshoes and eating heartily from the overabundance of meat. There was a pig in the ground, a whole side of beef and several chickens.

Soon, it was time for the toast. A bottle of Jack Daniels was passed forward while someone broke out the Dixie cups. The bride, barefoot in a red and white satin dress, with barbwire tattoo around her bicep was holding her Dixie cup in anticipation.

The groom meanwhile had picked up the top of the wedding cake and had walked stealthily toward her like a hunter stalking his prey. Suddenly from the shutter of my camera, I watched as cake was smashed into her face, hair, neck, and right ear.

Without missing a beat the bride swiped a handful of the next layer and smeared it into his camo vest. Within seconds, the bride and groom sported more frosting than the actual cake. 7 minutes later, (4 minutes longer than the ceremony) the bride and groom were still smearing cake, rolling on the grass, laughing and giggling, while the forgotten Jack Daniels sat dripping out the bottom of soggy Dixie cups.

I realize no girl wants a cookie cutter wedding...but this one took the cake...literally! I just hope there was insurance on the tuxes!

The Ford Zucchini 350

*C*lose the windows and lock the doors...the zucchini are coming! The much-maligned zucchini is already multiplying in gardens everywhere and soon the same old zucchini jokes will start making the rounds again. We laugh every year, but it's the desperate laugh of complicity.

One well-traveled zucchini joke is about the woman who grew the world's largest zucchini. On her way to show it to her friend, she stopped at the grocery store. Upon returning, she discovered something awful. Someone had left her the world's second largest zucchini too!

What is it about zucchini that germinates so many jokes? It's not the only vegetable in the garden that grows abundantly: there are usually more tomatoes, cucumbers and peppers. But who's ever heard a joke about too much corn, or too many peas?

My best guess is that it's in the nature of the plant itself. It really is the only plant that seems to produce its fruit nearly overnight. And you can't ever plant the right amount of zucchini. If you plant just one, it will die. If you plant two, you can feed the neighborhood. And no matter how often or how carefully you pick them, you will inevitably miss one, and within days it will become giant and tough.

Some people use these clubs for zucchini bread—but honestly, how much zucchini bread can one eat?

I have included one of my favorite recipes for those of you who have planted two zucchini plants and wish to remain on good terms with the neighbors. I call it the Zucchini FZ 350

Zucchini FZ 350

1 grocery bag of zucchini
1 raincoat
1 pair of sunglasses
1 moderately fast car

Directions:

Go to a busy feed store. Drive around until you find a pickup without a dog. Put the zucchini in the back and drive away fast!

Since the price of fuel this year has made the above recipe a little less cost effective (not to mention more people are hauling around their dogs) I have found another (even more sneaky) way to cope with the overabundance of zucchini. Pick off all the blossoms!

Zucchini
by Betty Rayl

I measured out my garden and I spaded up a plot
to plant a few green squash seeds, I didn't need a lot.
But when those plants began to grow, there must have been a genie
A lurkin' in the squash vines...you should see all my zucchini!

I've picked and packed and give away 'til my arms and back are sore.
But every time I turn around, there's always bushels more.
I have 2 dozen recipes, I can steam, fry, broil or bake,
or sneak them into soups or stews, or cookies, bread or cake.

The squash has worked me half to death. It's hard to say "I'm fine!"
My life would be much simpler, if they'd shrivel on the vine.
So may your troubles shrivel up, and may your blessings grow,
Like my bountiful zucchini in that tiny little row.

Good clean hunting

*I*t's hunting season again…a time for big game and bigger stories. And the wonderful thing about hunting stories is they don't have to be your own to tell them. One of my favorites took place several years before I was even born at my grandparents' home near Baker.

The weekend brought a houseful of hopeful hunters—filling the bedrooms and spilling over onto the furniture and floors. Each of the guests knew my grandparents but most were strangers to each other—but that didn't matter as they rolled out their sleeping bags next to future hunting buddies. My grandma's parents (my great-grandparents) had both come for the big weekend: my great-grandpa to hunt and maybe try out his homemade "corn wine," and my great-grandma to help with the cooking. The first night, the men came back with a deer that my great-grandma fixed them for breakfast the next morning.

The men had long since eaten and gone when my grandma stepped out of her room and was affronted by a terrible pungent odor. "What is that smell?" she asked her mom.

"Oh, I just made the men breakfast," my great-grandma replied.

"Well, what did you make?" my grandma asked, knowing that her mom sometimes liked to experiment with some of her more exotic seasonings when she visited.

"Just biscuits and gravy."

"Show me what you used," my grandma insisted, continuing to gag on the overwhelming smell.

"Well, I began by frying up the liver and heart with your new bottle of coconut oil..." she began.

"Coconut oil?" my grandma questioned. She didn't remember buying coconut oil. Beside the sink, sat the sack of yesterday's groceries she hadn't had time to put away yet. She picked up an opened bottle next to the sack. "You mean this bottle of coconut oil?" she asked, turning the bottle so my great-grandma could read the word that followed it... shampoo.

Between gasps of air, my great-grandma guffawed, "That would explain why the gravy foamed up so bad when I added the milk...oh no...and they slicked up every bite!"

The men didn't bring back a deer that night, and while they may have thought it had to do with imbibing in a little too much "corn wine," my grandma and her mom were putting their bets on the men's early morning "bubbly." They never did come clean, but they figured it was okay—the men were clean enough for both of them.

Dishes, pies, and visitors

*I*t seems to me that the amount of dirty dishes in your sink is directly proportional to the number of surprise guests that will just "pop in" for a quick visit. And I believe the reverse it also true: if your house is so clean you've dusted the top of the fridge and cleaned under the oven—you won't have one unexpected visitor.

Last week was busy. I was canning pearsauce, pepperoncinis, apples and freezing stuffed jalapeños and cream cheese pepper balls—all with the help of my toddler. Every pot, kettle, bowl and pitcher was filled with something in some stage of the preserving process—and the ones I wasn't using, my toddler had pulled out of the cupboard and filled with toys and utensils.

I had just pulled off a pepper soaked glove to push an obnoxious tendril of hair from my forehead, when my husband stepped through the kitchen door. He surveyed the huge mess then said flippantly: "Did you forget about the barbecue tonight?"

Oh. The barbecue. A birthday party for a friend. I looked around...a true kitchen nightmare: pots tipped haphazardly in the sink. Boxes with their vegetable remnants lay strewn on the floor, pepper juice dripped off the counter where the food processor and I had just had a misunderstanding.

The only thing missing was spaghetti hanging from the ceiling. My husband shrugged. "Just leave it—it's not like anyone's coming over..." So I pulled off my remaining glove, slipped out of my apron, and we headed in to the barbecue.

Two hours later, we returned from an enjoyable evening of roasted corn, hot dogs, and a delicious coconut cream pie. We were feeling stuffed, and I walked into the kitchen feeling even less excited about cleaning it—that is until I walked over to the stove—and found a beautiful apple pie sitting on the sticky ceramic burners. Suddenly, I had a surge of embarrassment-driven energy.

The kitchen was scrubbed from top to bottom that night. Every pan glistened and soon the only sign of canning was the neat rows of jars sitting on the pantry shelf. In the midst of all that cleaning, I discovered the best way to eliminate dirty dishes—eat out!

That was when my husband and I decided that the amount of dirty dishes in your sink is directly proportional to the number of surprise guests you will have—and shiny pans and clean dishes act as a human repellent—as we haven't had an unexpected guest since!!

A stranger's generosity

"*T*oy store!" my Little One squealed, as he and his dad arrived in the parking lot of the local hardware store. He went right over to the pedal tractors and began to drool. If anyone was curious to know what he's going to look like as an adult, just take my husband to a John Deere dealership; you'll notice the same glazed eyes, the same look of sincere passion, and of course the same drool leaking out the corner of his mouth. It's true what they say: "The only difference between men and boys, is the size and expense of their toys."

While my husband shopped, my Little One found a red, die-cast tractor to fix his affection on. (He's a little more color blind than his father.) "You should buy him one," a fellow shopper advised my husband. He smiled, shrugged, and they both continued shopping.

The lady met them again at the cash register. My Little One was still playing on the tractor, and she mentioned that her kids used to have one and loved it…maybe she should dig it out of the barn. "Would your little boy like it if I did?" What little boy wouldn't? They chatted a few minutes longer, then parted ways—a friendly meeting of strangers.

The chance meeting was interesting, but quickly forgotten. That is until last week, when a knock at my door, had me staring into the eyes of a blonde haired stranger. She couldn't remember my husband's first name, but remembered his last name. So she'd stopped by his dad's store, with the same last name, in the hopes of finding a relative. My father-in-law had given her directions to our house, and here she was, ready to give my Little One the tractor and trailer she'd dug out of her barn. A green tractor and trailer no less.

My mouth was dry. I was too surprised for words. She came and left before I had a chance to ask her name, or address, or pretty much anything. After a phone call to the hardware store, I found out what town she lived in, and that her last name is Fergusson, but still not enough information to send a card. So to the lady who made my Little One a very happy boy, thank you. We had never met before, and we may never meet again, but I am sure we will never forget you, or your surprising and generous gift.

Home & Gardening

If the shelves are dusty and the pots don't shine,
it's because I have better things to do with my time.

Multi-tasking with Windex

*A*s summer pressed into September, I began watching my garden very closely. I could hardly wait for the vegetables to ripen so that I could can. Although I must say I had an ulterior motive: as much as I love being up to my elbows in tomato paste and green bean fuzz—canning would get me out of the tractor seat.

Finally the day arrived bright and sunny—and I didn't have to enjoy it from behind a bug-stained windshield. Armed with grocery bags, boxes and Iliad, my dog, I began picking tomatoes and cucumbers, pulling up beets and kohlrabi and shucking corn.

When facing a busy afternoon, a competent woman knows that multi-tasking is the best way to tackle it. Being the competent woman I am, I tossed a basket of jeans in the washer, started the dishwasher, put a sheet of chili peppers on to broil, filled a double steamer with corn, and began the task of boiling tomatoes to remove their skins.

The problem a competent woman faces with multi-tasking, is that sooner or later, everything will simultaneously demand attention. This became evident when the faucet started leaking (I guess I hadn't tightened it enough during installation last week). I had barely gotten out the pliers, when the timer on my corn buzzed. Setting down the pliers, I set the steamed corn aside and refilled the steamer with more raw ears of corn. By now my tomatoes had boiled themselves to almost mush. I quickly transferred what was left to a bowl of ice water, and put more fresh tomatoes in to boil.

Forgetting the faucet, I checked my peppers in the oven—or should I say what was left of the peppers in the oven. It seems I had overcooked them until I had a sheet of pepper-shaped charcoal. I pulled on rubber gloves and tried to salvage the remains. As I pushed the last "pepper" into a freezer bag, my cat began throwing up on the rug behind me. I grudgingly reached for the mop. Suddenly my pot of tomatoes boils over, only to be surpassed by the loud buzz from the corn steamer...and the dryer timer...not to mention the faucet.

With all of those demands, I did what any competent woman would do. I grabbed a bottle of Windex and two rolls of shop towels—bug stains on tractor windshields can be awfully stubborn.

Diet books and France

I read somewhere that the two most popular books sold are cookbooks and diet books. Cookbooks teach you how to prepare the gourmet food that diet books teach you not to eat.

Now I personally am not inclined to buy either—for if left to my own cooking, I would eat popcorn and V8 juice every day. I know this as fact, for in college, my sister and I survived on popcorn and dates (and I don't mean the fruit).

I do enjoy baking on occasion, and am actually fairly decent in the kitchen—as long as it doesn't include making cookies. Elly Mae Clampett has nothing on me when it comes to cookies. My family refers to my attempts as "Oreo cookies"—black on the outside and doughy in the middle.

Lucky for me, I married a farmer who frequently hangs up his greasy farm cap for a chef's hat. The deal we've made is he cooks, I clean up—and we both benefit from not eating popcorn for breakfast.

We just recently visited Europe, and my personal chef was very interested in the French cuisine. It seems like there's always a new book on the market about how the French can consume such rich food and wine and still remain attractively thin. And my husband was eager to discover their secret ingredient and adopt it into his recipes.

Once there, we sampled many of their dishes, both entrees and desserts—and they were just as tasty as expected. And before we left, we had discovered their secret of staying thin—they walk all over the country.

If Americans would walk as much as the French, we could maintain our current fast-food lifestyle and people would be writing books about us, wondering how we stay so slim. So, the uncovered secret, alas, is that same as always...exercise. Either that or eat popcorn three meals a day.

Headaches & home remedies

I have spent a good portion of my life battling headaches. I will lay in bed with the blinds drawn, ice packs on my head, praying I will be able to keep down the Excedrin. The headaches last anywhere from a few hours to a couple of days. But eventually they will subside and I return to the land of the living where I will be bombarded with home remedies from caring friends and devious relatives.

Some are practical, like 'drink more water,' or 'eat less fried food,' while others run into the macabre of coffee enemas—did they forget it was the top of me that hurts—not the bottom? Sometimes it is even more unusual than that. I was once given a 'cure' that said to "put 3 drops of the tincture of blood root into half a glass of water and take 2 teaspoonfuls every 15 minutes until relieved. It sounds like Dracula's favorite salad dressing. Even if I was inclined to try it, what in tarnation is blood root, and where does one go about obtaining it?

Friends are always sending me recipes that call for medicines I've never heard of like Nux Comica, pheacetin, spigelia, and bromide of potash. And while at one point in time these ingredients may have been grown in the family garden—my garden is mostly overrun with squash.

This last Christmas, my mom received a giant book of modern day home remedies. She spent the remainder of the day 'curing' all of our ailments from gall bladder attacks to acne. Her eyes lit up when she hit upon headache remedies. While many were mundane (and sounded nice), like soaking your feet in hot water with ice packs on your head, my mom found one that she was sure would work for me.

Pour a bit of cayenne pepper into the palm of your hand and snort it up your nose! I didn't try it, but I'm sure it works...like breaking your leg to alleviate the pain of a sprained finger. Or my dad's cure to anything...got a stubbed toe or hay allergies? Amputation at the neck solves it all. Thanks guys, but next time I have a headache, I think I'll take an aspirin and call in sick.

Light bulbs, questions, & men

*H*ow many men does it take to change a light bulb? This is not a trick question. Think back to your childhood. The kitchen light was out, who changed it—mom or dad? And if it was your dad, was he ever unsupervised? Let me digress for just a moment while you think back.

Earlier this year, I had a harebrained idea to paint the bathroom. To do a good job, I needed the metal soap dish removed from the tub. Unfortunately, the screws were rusty—and stripped out with little pressure. After a couple of minutes of frustration, I figured this was a good job for my husband. When he came home, I handed him a drill, a screwdriver and his assignment. Only minutes had passed before "dadblastit!!" was shouted through the open bathroom door.

My husband stood in the tub, a hammer in one hand, a cats paw in the other and a big hole in the shower. Behind him, the soap dish remained firmly attached to the wall. I ended up having to remove the dish myself (which I should have done to begin with!)

Eight months with a hole the size of a basketball in the shower was enough—I was going to fix it if it meant patching it together with bubble gum and baler twine! I had barely gotten started, when my husband decided to help.

Instead of trying to match tiles to fix the hole, he believed it would be better if we just replaced all the tiles on the back wall (to which I agreed—anything to get the hole fixed!) "It won't be much harder to replace the Sheetrock while we're at it—it'll make a more solid base for the new tile anyway," he added.

So the Sheetrock came down. Then it was the insulation that needed replacing . Since we were that far, "we may as well install a new window." And now would be a good time to update the plumbing "since we're this far along anyway..."

Before I could really comprehend was happening, the original 13-inch hole now had engulfed the entire bathroom. He was now making plans to replace all the walls, putting in a new bathtub and replacing the flooring. I've been washing my hair in the kitchen sink for two weeks now—all because I wanted to paint the bathroom.

This brings me back to my original question. How many men does it take to change a light bulb? I'm not sure anyone really knows, because by the time you have re-tiled the floors, replaced the windows, painted the walls, and put in a new stove and sink—the light bulb that needed changing has been replaced by skylights.

(I admit women aren't much better at changing light bulbs—but our attempts rarely include remodeling ventures.)

I just ate my willpower

I've read somewhere that willpower is being able to eat just one salted peanut. Recently, I decided to put this theory to the test. I very proudly ate just one salted peanut. I thought about eating another one, but instead congratulated myself as I tightened the jar lid and put the peanuts back in the cupboard.

Since I had done so well with the peanuts, I decided to test myself again...I pulled out the can of Pringles. Only one chip, then I returned the can to the shelf. Boy, this willpower thing is easy. I was batting 100. One garlic baby dill pickle, one olive, one baby carrot, one macadamia nut cookie, and one scoop of cottage cheese. I opened the freezer. Surely there was something in here that I could use to keep testing this wonderfully strong willpower of mine. As luck would have it, there was—one spoonful each of orange sherbert and bunny tracks ice cream. One frozen peppermint patty and a raspberry push-up.

All that ice cream left me craving something salty. I looked through the cupboards. One BBQ chip, one jalapeno chip, one salt and vinegar chip, and one Dorito. I had just decided to conclude the test on my amazing willpower, when my eyes lit upon that jar of peanuts. My mouth started watering. I could almost taste the nutty flavor. I lifted the jar and caressed the lid. Oh, I wanted one more. Maybe, if...I slammed the cupboard door on my peanut temptation.

Later that evening, my husband came home. "What in the world?" he stammered, looking around at empty potato chip bags and half empty bowls of ice cream and piles of candy wrappers. I proudly held up the full jar of peanuts. "Look Honey, I only ate one!"

Nutrition for dummies

$\mathcal{B}$ack when I was little, eating right didn't seem to be a problem. You simply ate what was put on your plate—in its entirety—if you didn't, you would eat it again later for your next meal. Once after refusing to eat gooey oatmeal with swollen raisins for breakfast, my mother made good on that threat. I discovered that no matter how gross raisin oatmeal is, it is much more gross for lunch. After that, I decided that while it may not be good the first time around—it's a WHOLE lot worse the second. Thus eating right, meant eating what was put on my plate.

Lately though, it seems a whole lot more complicated. Everyone seems to be undergoing a new diet. Now remember, my resolution was to eat seconds…not diet. Unfortunately for me, my chef/husband decided it was his turn to climb on board the diet wagon.

While I support him 100%, I am selfishly frustrated. I have become so dependent on his cooking, that this last week, I will open the fridge and stare at its contents, hoping that they will somehow just jump together and fill my empty bowl with something edible. So far, I've had no luck scrambling eggs with telekinesis but I think I have shortened the life expectancy of our milk by keeping the door open so long.

For a couple of days it seemed I was back to college fare: popcorn and V8 juice. But somehow that didn't seem right, with my husband on a diet...I needed to find something more nutritious—and easy to prepare.

According to an article I recently read, I discovered eating right doesn't have to be complicated. Nutritionists say there is a simple way to tell if you're eating right. Colors. Fill your plates with bright colors. Greens, reds, yellows.

How easy is that? I was so excited to try out my new idea, I started yesterday morning. I had an entire bowl of Skittles. It was delicious! I never knew eating right could be so easy. I now have a whole new outlook on nutrition.

Fireworks & potato salad

*O*ne afternoon, waiting for my midwife, I perused a few parenting magazines with articles such as "Why baby won't eat his food," and "How will big brother relate to baby?" I wasn't interested, there wasn't a big brother, and if anyone ever bothered to taste baby food, they'd know exactly why baby doesn't want to eat his canned, pureed, vegetable goo.

But one article did catch my attention. It discussed how a baby dealt with noise. The author said if you didn't want your baby to be startled easily then you had to get them acclimatized to sudden and loud noises. The article recommended vacuuming the nursery during nap time and not quieting the barking dog. This was new to me; most mothers start shushing people if their baby even begins to look sleepy. The articles went on to say that even during the last few months of pregnancy you should experience the sounds you want your baby to be familiar with.

It must have worked, I never gave up driving tractor through the pregnancy, and was still driving one the afternoon he was born. And interestingly enough, machinery noise doesn't bother my baby, neither does the dog or the vacuum, and he only causally glances at the air wrenches in Les Schwab.

All was good until the Fourth of July. We were planning on attending the fireworks in my hometown. I was really concerned about the loud sonic booms—the blinding flash of white followed by a thundering clap. I waited with nervous anticipation—I just knew those would be too much for his little 5-month-old ears. Dusk finally fell, and as we lay there on the grass, my baby started to rub his eyes. Before the grand finale he was sound asleep. Sleeping soundly through all the sonic booms. I was so proud of him (and myself for acclimatizing him to loud noises).

Just as my head was beginning to swell, I decided to make some potato salad. I dumped pickles into my kitchen chopper and hit start. My baby jerked so hard, he nearly fell out of his bouncer. Tears began gushing amidst panicked gulps and ear piercing shrieks. Too late I remember the part of the article that said they had to be accustomed to the noise, preferably in the womb. And I was in the kitchen. With as much cooking as I do, the only kitchen gadget he was familiar with would probably be the fork!

Fast and furious

*F*ast food, faster Internet, fast cars, 4G networks and people on the fast track to fame and fortune: everything worth owning, knowing or driving seems to be fast.

Long winter nights with mother knitting in the rocker, father reading under the newspaper, and the kids playing with Rover while listening to episodes of "The Shadow" are a thing of the past, only to be read about in Norman Rockwell memoirs.

A more likely scenario for today's winter nights put the father on a cellphone, hunched over a computer and furiously clicking on the mouse. The mother has dinner cooking in the microwave, the PTA president on the phone planning the next school fund-raiser, all the while scheduling a dentist appointment on her Blackberry. Meanwhile, the kids are trying out Olympics bobsledding on the Wii; and Rover has been traded in for a more economic fish that doesn't eat pounds of food or require walks during favorite TV shows.

The speed at which our society is racing through life can easily be seen in our pop culture. Everywhere you look— billboards, magazine covers, TV advertisements, radio jingles—you find slogans like: "fast acting," "if you call in the next 10 minutes…," "dinners in under 30 minutes," "just add water," and "drop 3 pant sizes in 2 weeks." Our culture is full of things like speed reading, instant pudding and drive through divorce courts.

We seem to live in a state of fast forward—especially during the holidays. The hustle and bustle was never more apparent than while staying at a friend's house in Vancouver. My girlfriend and I had convinced our husbands to watch our babies while we did some shopping. The guys weren't quite as excited as we were about this little excursion so we knew we better leave before they changed their minds!

My girlfriend went rushing off to get ready. Less than 5 minutes later she comes downstairs, showered, dressed, hair done and sporting eye shadow! Gaping at her speed, she shrugged her shoulders, "I was in a hurry…. I didn't use soap." Ahh…You know, speed isn't all it's cracked up to be.

I'd say the moral is to stop and smell the roses—but they were traded in for Glade plug-ins months ago—the scent travels faster.

Childlike awe & pizza

*E*ssayist, novelist and poet G.K. Chesterton once said, "When it comes to life the critical thing is whether you take things for granted or take them with gratitude." Never has this been brought into focus so much to me, as grocery shopping this week.

I have traveled around the world and seen people living in mud huts, stayed in homes without running water, eaten food that is full of vermin, and seen half-naked children play with garbage bags tied up with strings to make balls. Each time I go somewhere, I have always come home, happy to live in the United States.

But this week I saw my country through new eyes. I picked up a friend from the airport on his first visit to the States. He was surprised how long it took to drive from Portland to the east side of Oregon. He startled me when he said he'd never been in a car ride that long. He could drive across his country (of Majuro) in 45 minutes. Wow. I breathed deeply in the open air that I'd always taken for granted.

The week before his visit, I had been very busy putting on a Vacation Bible School for our church, and hadn't made it to the grocery store. My fridge looked like it should have belonged to a college student. Mayonnaise, mustard and ketchup bottles were all alone except for a half-eaten jar of pickles, a cream cheese package and an empty orange juice carafe. A grocery run was necessary.

The produce section stunned my friend. "Look at all the vegetables!" he kept exclaiming. "I noticed him standing in front of the plastic wrapped melon slice. "Ooooh," he grinned, pointing. "And look at the price! 78 cents!"

"I know," I agreed, shaking my head. He looked up. "I think it's great!" It wasn't long before his camera came out. "Everything's so cheap! The cauliflower's under $4...look at the strawberries...I paid $5 for a case that size last week... wow, Doritos are under $2!, they are over $5 for me..." So the dialogue continued: cheese, bread, crackers, chocolate, butter, melons, grapes, lettuce, carrots....

During a supper of fresh pizza, he couldn't stop commenting on the freshness of the tomatoes. The whole situation left me feeling odd. I had seen poverty in other countries, but I had really never stopped to ponder the wealth and quantity of my own. Maybe his excitement will give me fresh eyes to see even common things such as a grocery store or pizza with more appreciation.

Dinner anyone?

I really like food. I love smelling food, I love buying food and I love eating food. I don't, however, enjoy cooking food. Most of my friends know I made it though college on popcorn, V8 and Saturday night dinner dates. My time in the kitchen is best spent canning, cleaning, or doing art projects on the table. My cooking fiascoes started early in life. After making a few batches of "Oreo" cookies (black on the outside, gooey in the middle), my family began comparing my cooking results with Elly May's biscuits off the Beverly Hillbillies. I can turn a ball of cookie dough to a briquette faster than Lisa Douglas could bubble up one of her hotcakes Oliver uses to reshingle their Hootersville shack.

I must say I come by it naturally though. I recall a time my grandma tried her hand at a "dump casserole." A casserole where you dump in whatever happens to be in your fridge. Well, my grandma, bless her heart, took it too literally. Lettuce and peanut butter stood glommed together as she scraped the inedible goo into the dog dish. I think the dog ate out that night. I know we did.

I like to bake, but that day-to-day cooking is a struggle for me. Although, now with a little boy in the house, I feel obligated to feed him more than popcorn. So lately I've been making daily excursions to the kitchen. Unfortunately, the kitchen is close to 3 smoke detectors, which my husband affectionately refers to as my oven timers. Hopefully in case of a real fire, the family will head outside and not to the table.

I'm just waiting for the day my 3-year-old heads outside to make mud pies and the rest of the family take their forks and follow. But there are upsides, relatives don't stay any longer than necessary, friends invite us to make the dinner mess at their house, and I can get even with anyone—with only a "home-cooked meal" and a smile.

Family

Don't judge folks by their relatives.

That's not what I meant

$\mathcal{E}$ach family has its very own dialect of words, phrases and definitions. My family's jargon has come to include words we found to be funny, words we mispronounced as children, or other odd words we've adopted from friends, books, or our travels.

Gramma Scabetty had always seemed normal in lieu of Grandma Betty; Puh Guh, Guh, for PGG, goulash for noodles with vegetables. I had never stopped to think that sometimes my family jargon might not be clearly decipherable—until this summer. After spending most of one day in the swather, the fuel gauge was beginning to beep at me. I called up my husband, and after a few pleasantries I told him I was "out of go-go juice." That is common Walker terminology for being out (or nearly out) of diesel, gas, or propane. "No problem," he said, "I can be out there in about 30 minutes or so."

He did arrive in the given time period—with a bottle of water and a bag of potato chips.

Another instance of understanding the words but not the meaning, happened last year while visiting my sister in the West Indies. One evening her roommate (from Oregon) was putting together a desk, and asked if someone would hand her "a plus." My husband and I were baffled. She tried to explain, "You know, the opposite of a minus." Still confused, she stood up and got herself a plus, known to us as a Philips screwdriver

And then there are the strange words that somehow just slipped into our family's vocabulary. One of my favorites is Woahink. We encountered that on a family vacation a few years back. "Woa hink bad" someone said while pinching their nose. "Wwwhhoooa Hink!" someone else said holding up their hand like a traffic cop. "Wooaaa hinnnnkkkk..." someone else lamented. From that moment on, Woahink is one of those Walker words that can take on any definition to fit any circumstance. Very similar to the more familiar "oh."

During a phone conversation "oh" can be used to express surprise, delight, suspicion, astonishment, and boredom. Woahink can do the same thing with a bit more flair. Try it sometime—Woahink?

Family tree sap

$\mathcal{E}$very tree has a little sap in it…and that is especially true with the family tree. Having just survived the holiday season…I can attest firsthand to that! One never can be sure what to expect when all the aunts and uncles, cousins and grandchildren start arriving for the family festivities. Even when you think you're prepared…it starts flooding and you haven't even collected half of the gopher wood needed for the ark!!

This year was no exception. Braced for loud, raucous laughing and slightly off-color if not hilarious jokes, it was weird, to find the turkey on the table, the relatives talking quietly in the living room and everything unusually normal. Dinner was nearly ready, only one thing left to do… chop the jalapeños. Before I knew it, I had a knife in one hand and a bowl of peppers in the other.

Misery loves company, so I snagged my cousin and soon we were trying to top one another's tales. We were nearly finished when my grandma noticed we hadn't removed the seed cavity. So with feigned grumbles we began cutting out the seeds.

Our laughter quickly resumed until my cousin started to fuss about her nose. It was turning fiery red. Pepper oil is lethal on skin, and she had touched her nose with jalapeño fingers. The only thing I knew that would stop the burning is to soak the affected skin in milk. Too bad grandma didn't have any…but no worries…she did have sour cream!

I couldn't help but giggle as the aunties bustled around my cousin smearing her whole face with white cream. The cream was dribbling down her face as fast as they could smear it on. After using a good portion of the carton, they decided it wasn't working.

But no worries…grandma also had ice cream! It has milk enzymes in it! Now it wasn't just me guffawing, many of my cousins were standing around watching the aunties goober her face with French vanilla bean!! Now, in addition to white creamy streaks, she had big frozen globs dotted with cute brown speckles. The laughter was running as fast as the ice cream. Unfortunately, my cousin's nose was even more inflamed than ever.

Soon, the aunties started tossing around ideas that sounded like the start of a crazy kitchen science experiment. Just then, my husband remembered we had two buckets of fresh jersey milk in the back of our pickup. I think he brought it in less out of mercy, and more because he wanted to watch her dip her whole face in a five-gallon bucket of raw milk! And for the record, Cindy Crawford's milk mustache has nothing over the full-face dip!!

Thankfully, the milk enzymes diffused the pepper oil, and her face started returning to its normal hue. But not before many Kodak moments were created!

And you know, I've decided I don't mind a little sap after all…no family…er…tree would be alive without it!!

Dad-approved day care

I admired my shiny blue snowmobile while I pulled on my helmet and tightened my gloves. With one quick pull, the engine began to rumble. As the snow flurried around my face, I suddenly had a flashback to my childhood.

There was a light skiff of snow on the ground, and one of my best friends and I were hovering over an old snowmobile. We were so excited, not only did Hermiston have snow on the ground, but we had permission to ride one of my dad's snowmobiles. There was only one catch. He didn't have time to start it for us…so if we wanted to ride it…we had to start it.

We had the hood up, and my friend's job was to spray the ether and hold the throttle while I pulled the rope. We spent the entire afternoon crossing our fingers and begging the machine to start. After using two bottles of ether and a bottle of WD40 for good measure (neither of which worked), we decided there wasn't enough snow anyway. We'd had fun….just like we always did every time we tried to start that old thing.

Boy, those were good times. I pulled my visor down and revved up my engine…it's nice not to depend on ether…but when I have kids, (as much as I love the roar of the engine), I'm going to smile as I pocket the spark plugs and hand them a case of ether….

Signs of adulthood

*D*riving home from a parts run, I had the startling sensation of becoming a "grown-up." I've traveled around the world, graduated from college, taught high school, and had a baby—and none of those things made me feel as old as I did pulling up next to a stoplight beside a couple of teenagers. Every window in their car was open. I glanced at my mirror thermometer: 34 F.

The kids were wearing sweatshirts and stocking caps, and I shivered involuntarily as I turned up the heater. What is it about driving around with the windows down that is "cool?" I enjoy driving with the windows down too—in the summer! But I admit it wasn't too many years ago that all my windows would have been down too—rain or snow—because it was cool. I never realized those days had passed, but now I'm more concerned with cold than cool.

Later that week, I was riding with my sister and telling her how old I felt with my windows shut up tight. After a couple of minutes trying to shout over her music and repeating "What?" I reached over and turned the car's radio down. She gave me one of those "young" looks that quite plainly expressed it wasn't just rolling up the windows that made me old.

I guess you know you're an adult when you become sensitive to the temperature–and you realize the volume button turns to the left.

What's in your vending machine?

*W*hat would you do with a million dollars? No doubt we've all asked ourselves that question, but what if you really had to put an answer down on paper? Looking around the group of family and friends, I pondered my answer a minute more, then scribbled my response on a scrap of paper.

Eggnog came out my brother's nose as we read some of our answers. "I would buy all of my "favorite people" a one-way ticket to Tanzania." "I would divide it up into $5 Wal-Mart gift cards," and "I would create a vaccine against stupid." Our game night was just beginning.

I believe that you can learn more about someone in 5 minutes of play, than in 5 hours of polite conversation. And that night our learning curve was steep!

The next question asked us what things you shouldn't teach your parrot. Polly said a lot of unrepeatables during that round; the less-offensive included "Fat butt. You have a big, fat butt," and "You looked better yesterday."

Wow...I couldn't believe our group was coming up with

these answers—this was better than stand up comedy!

What shouldn't you do at a job interview? "Beg for money." What things shouldn't you yell at the top of your lungs? "Let's make babies," or "I have pinworms." What kinds of things shouldn't you do in a theater? "Eat popcorn off the floor," "Dance in front," and my personal favorite "Get caught."

The questions just kept evoking bizarre answers from our group. What kinds of things shouldn't you put in your front yard? "A tent for the in-laws," "A giant personal ad—next to the couch your wife left you." "Your step-mama's mobile home," and "Pee resistant manikins!" As the game progressed we pondered things we wouldn't want to find in our beds, (our hot date's wig), and things that make you feel your age (opening a can of food for the cat and you wind up eating a "tuna" sandwich).

But the favorite question of the evening asked: What things do you wish you could buy out of vending machines? I never knew how primitive vending machines were—until I heard our answers: "Interest on your money," "new tractors," "the perfect girl," and "spouse shutter-uppers." Wow!

After a few hours of painful hysterics, we finally closed the lid on our box of "Things," but not before I'd decided two things: 1. Jeff Foxworthy doesn't have the monopoly on redneck...not with your step-mama's mobile home in the front yard next to your pee-resistant gnomes.

And 2: I'm never leaving my baby boy alone with them for long periods of time...If their *birds* say things like "You looked better yesterday," who knows what my *baby* will come home parroting!!

Moo + moo = chocolate?

*W*hen is a farmer like a magician? When he turns cows into moose. Let me explain. It was game night in the Walker house; which is always both entertaining and enlightening. The evening's game selection was Cloodle—similar to Pictionary. It was my dad's turn to draw. He picks up a card, the timer turns over, his pencil hovers over the paper…and nothing happens. Finally his face screws up, "I've never heard of this before."

Now, unlike Pictionary, Cloodle provides a hint to accompany each item to draw. The clue provided for this one was 'food.' The timer's still going, so we tell him to draw it in pieces. He's still looking confused. My sister and I exchange "oh boy" glances while we start thinking of puzzling types of food that he would be unfamiliar with. I shout out the first one that pops into my head: "Moo shu gai pan!" I don't think my dad knew if I was speaking in tongues of if he should wash my mouth out. Regardless, it was a 'no' as far as the game was concerned.

Suddenly, he pointed his pencil and you could see an idea forming. "Ya, what did you say?" he asked me. Moo Shu? He starts nodding vigorously—and begins to draw stick figure cows. I repeat Moo, my sister says Shoe and my mom pipes up with cows. He points at me: I say moo. He points at my mom: she says cow. His pencil points faster and faster: "cow moo, moo cow, moo moo." He's nodding like a bobble dog. So we repeat "moo moo moo moo," like a bunch of mad cows singing 'Old McDonald.' Just as the last sand is about to fall, someone yelled chocolate mousse!

My dad had broken it down...just like we told him to. And in the process we learned four valuable things: 1. The plural of moo is chocolate moose. 2. Since neither my dad nor brother knew what chocolate mousse was—we, as a family, need to eat more dessert. 3. Chocolate answers most things. And lastly, 4: The family that moos together—becomes laughing stock.

By the short hairs

I have a big mouth. And I don't mean in a Julia Roberts' smile sort of way. Now, there are several benefits to this... no one ever has to ask what I'm thinking...and I rarely feel the need to lie on a couch and spill my guts—because I never stop spilling them. Unfortunately though, there is one pretty large downside: I get to chew on my shoes frequently—and sometimes the shoes aren't just mine....

There have been many occasions in my life when I would have benefited from keeping my laughter to myself—but one time in particular stands out. I was in my late teens, and my cousin and I were sitting across the Subway table from our two dates. I can't recall their names or what the rest of our date entailed—but there was one hairy moment that will haunt me all the days of my life.

The conversation was dull, and my cousin began slowly running her hand across her neck and face, in a classic "I'm bored" gesture, when she suddenly began wiping at something on her chin. She soon leaned over to me and asked me if there was a hair tickling her chin. She turned her profile into the sunlight and I reach over to brush the pesky thing away. That's when she yelped—the hair was attached!

My big mouth couldn't stop chortling—as she pushed

over me trying to make an escape to the ladies room. I followed, telling her this was nothing to "pull her hair out over"...I mean just because she was having one "bad hair day." Standing in front of the mirror, I began pantomiming her discovery in the restaurant, when I stopped mid-breath. My cousin glanced over, noticing my pallid complexion, my hand on my chin, and moved in for the kill. Yes, she had me "by the hair on my chinny chin chin."

I tried to tell her that at least mine was shorter...but she told me I was "splitting hairs." That was when I first began to realize just how big my mouth was, but I guess it's no use tearing one's hair out over it...after all both traits are 'inhairited.'

Oh be careful little eyes what you...hear?

$\mathcal{S}$ometimes my mouth goes faster than my brain. You've been there: seconds after a thought leaves your mouth you realize what you've said. Given another second you could have said it better, but once it's out you have to live with the consequences.

How is it that your mouth can work faster than your brain? There needs to be a gear reduction mechanism in your brain that will prevent the output (speech) from exceeding input (thought). A device like that could prevent gaffes like: "What time does the 7 o'clock ferry leave?" or "How do I tell the difference between the big staples and the little staples?"

One of my favorite examples of this was years ago—long before caller ID, and children with cellphones. My grandma called us up on our home phone and was chatting about her day, when she paused and excused herself for a moment. She came back on the phone with this explanation: "I thought I heard you at my door!"

It's bad enough to say dumb things...but sometimes they

get into print! I recently saw a sign on a gym door that read "Do not open this door when locked!" and seen on a road sign: "Caution! Water on road during rain."

And worse still is if you're famous, and you say something less than brilliant, it will be stuck to your name forever; like the quote attributed to Gerald Ford saying "Things are more like they are now than they have ever been."

Even if you're not famous, you still may say things that will be with you forever. My dad made one of those forever comments last Saturday night. The game: "The Weakest Link." The venue: my parent's dining room table. The question read "Besides hearing, what other function does the ear perform?" He paused a split second before shouting out "Smell!"

I've heard of maximizing potential...but wow! I wonder what the rest of his senses do? He doesn't need the Three Wise Monkeys...he can probably cover his ears, and block out his mouth and ears all at once! I bet the evening would have gone different if he'd have had a gear reduction mechanism!

The night's frivolities gave us deep insight into men. The next time the man you're with doesn't seem to be listening...be patient...he may just be smelling the roses—and men aren't known for multi-tasking!

Weddings & sundaes

*T*he cake was ready, the guests were seated, the bouquets finished, and the groom was standing alone on the platform...it was time.

Nervous anticipation flowed through my fingers, making it difficult to hold my camera steady. It was time.

Just as the absence was becoming noticeable, a familiar little blonde appeared at the end of the aisle runner toting a very large Bible chalked full of notes and papers. My baby's first appearance as a Bible Boy.

At not quite 2, and having missed rehearsal, I had no idea what kind of performance to expect.

My pride ballooned with each step as he trotted down the isle, carrying his oversize load. He made a beeline straight for me, on the front row—handed me the Bible—then quickly turned heel and trucked back down the aisle, passing the flower girl halfway!

Weddings are such interesting times. No matter how much planning, or preparations they never seem to be perfect—unless they're scripted on a big screen—but even Hollywood has retakes to make those moments magical!

I think that all the weird quirks just make for more colorful stories.

This wedding was no exception. The best story happened to my cousin-in-law on the 8-hour drive to the wedding. She was riding in the back of an SUV with who I'll call Great Aunt Gertie (you know who she is…every family has one).

First they stopped for hot dogs…soon my cousin-in-law asked for napkins…because Aunt Gertie had made quite a statement with the ketchup and mustard.

But it was nothing compared to the ice cream sundaes they picked up later. It wasn't long before the front seat heard gagging noises from back.

Figuring it had something to do with Aunt Gertie, the front seat discreetly texted the back seat, asking what was wrong.

The reply text? "Gertie just took out her teeth to lick off the ice cream!" Talk about licking your chops!

Weddings and families! You have to love their unexpected quirks. And no matter how hard you try to hide them in your family tree foliage—every family has a few fruits and nuts.

Now, if only we could get that recipe for Applets and Cotlets!

A peck of peppered peaches

I don't remember exactly what the fight was over. Something about the news, or the newscaster, or the station it was on—either way it was a non sequitur for the events that followed, and the memory it made. It was breakfast, and I was going to be late for school if I didn't hurry. I had just finished up, when my grandpa spooned himself another bowl of peaches. I should have been tying my shoes and filling my backpack, but my grandparents fights were always so fun to watch…so I helped myself to another bowl of peaches too.

The fight continued. Now, to clarify things a bit; this was not a yelling fight, or a fight whose outcome would make any difference to either of them, or even a fight where they were angry with each other. It was simply, as my grandmother would later tell me, "two very vocal people who had two differing views of opinion." Their "opinions" kept getting more heated, and yet if one would have turned off the sound, all one would have seen was my grandpa, head down, slowly, methodically, eating his peaches.

Suddenly, something out of the ordinary happened. My grandma, again without any big flourishes, walked over to my grandpa, picked up the pepper shaker, and unloaded it into his bowl of peaches. "Hmph," she said, as she walked back into the kitchen. That seemed to be the closing period on their "discussion." I was snorting, and sneezing, and holding my stomach from laughter pain. But my grandpa didn't even crack a smile. I'm not even sure he missed a bite of peaches. He just kept rhythmically spooning them to his lips. After a couple of peppered bites, he offered an epilogue, "You know you ruined these peaches don't you?" But that didn't stop him from eating every last piece of fruit in his bowl.

By now, I am all but lying on the floor rolling, I have tears pouring down my cheeks, and I'm starting to gasp for air. This was their best fight yet. But there was still more to come. As soon as my grandpa finished the peaches, my grandma bustled in and took the bowl to the sink. He stood up, and headed for the door. My grandma followed him out on the porch, where I expected to hear a continuation of their argument. Instead, I stared in amazement as I saw their silhouettes start to smooch.

When my grandma came back in, she took note of my bewildered look and explained: "One never knows what will happen throughout the day. Grandpa may go off to work and something could happen—to him—or to me. And I don't want our last memory to be a fight. So we always take the opportunity to kiss goodbye."

I was late for school that day, but I'm not sure that any geometry or biology lesson could have topped the two life lessons I learned that day: 1. Peppered peaches can be eaten with a straight face 2. Make sure all your fights are non sequiturs.

Politics

"The farmer is the only man in our economy who buys everything at retail, sells everything at wholesale, and pays the freight both ways."

~John F. Kennedy

Elections and chickens

*W*ith elections right around the corner, my mailbox seems to be bombarded by myriad flyers, newsletters, and campaign brochures all promoting different candidates. Two things amuse me about these advertisements: the pictures, and the quotes.

The pictures portray the candidate in the foreground while the background hosts barns, vegetables, tractors, windmills and other agricultural implements. The quotes usually say something along the lines of promoting the state's agriculture and being in tune to the farmers and ranchers of America.

While I also advocate for the support of America's farmers and ranchers, I still just have to wonder. What percentage of the candidates' time is actually spent in the fields, shaking hands with ranchers, and driving tractors? And what percent is spent out of the fields, shaking hands with white collars, and driving vehicles without 3-point hitches?

When I was little, my parents used to read me a story about a little hen. Planting season arrived, but found her friends too busy to help her sow the grain. She blithely replied "I guess I'll go and do it by myself." Harvest came and went, and still her friends were too busy to help. On her way to the field with a sickle she said "I guess I'll go and do it by myself."

The same thing happened when it came time to thresh the wheat, and then again when it was time to bake the bread.

But no sooner had the oven timer rung, when her friends were at the door, tummies rumbling. She stretched out her little neck and sing-songed, "I planted the wheat by myself, I harvested the wheat by myself, I threshed the wheat by myself, I baked the wheat by myself. So I guess I'll go and eat it by myself."

Just as the tummies started to rumble when the bread was done, so the farmer in everyone starts to come out when the voters pamphlets are done. To be clear, I'm not saying the candidates are not sincere in their claims. But I would like to leave you with one final thought. Does parking in a garage make you a car? Does standing in a hanger make you an airplane? Neither does standing in front of agricultural products make you a farmer.

Voting headaches

*M*y head was throbbing by the fourth page into Measure 49. I believe in order to write laws or other government documents, one must first attend special classes to learn to write run-on sentences. I had made it through the first three sections okay and then I started section 4. The first sentences contained 107 words, 4 commas, and a lot of uncertainty.

If I had submitted a sentence like that to one of my English professors, I am certain they would have handed it right back and reminded me I was in a college-level class. And, as if run-on sentences weren't enough, Measure 49 included 22 sections and had nearly 14,000 words!

I massaged my forehead and tried to plow through the remaining sections containing parcel lot numbers, sea levels, slopes, percentages and cubic feet of wood fibers. Soon I gave up, and started just skimming. Anyone who has ever tried simply perusing a state measure knows just how futile that is. I gained nothing from the last 15 pages—save for a worsening headache.

I read the explanatory statement, and decided I needed more explanation—perhaps the arguments would help. Yes, it will help the farmer develop his land—no, it will allow the government to take your property without compensation.

Yes it will—no it won't. Ahhhh. My headache was quickly turning into a migraine!

After spending the entire evening waffling back and forth on the measure, I began wondering whether voting without knowledge was worse than not voting at all. I really wanted to vote for the best option...unfortunately, like most elections, the best option wasn't on the ballot.

I took two aspirin on my way to bed, and had a frightening thought: If Measure 49 was this difficult to see through, next year's presidential election was going to be brutal. I better stock up on cold compresses and Excedrin.

Frivolous lawsuits, creative results

*O*ur country is bombarded with frivolous lawsuits: women suing over spilled coffee, burglars suing over injuries obtained while falling through skylights, and myriad other instances.

I recently came across the following tale, and while it probably isn't true, it at least gives us hope that in this overly litigious society plagued by frivolous lawsuits and scams, justice does prevail and that clever crimes have equally clever consequences.

A lawyer purchased a box of very rare and expensive cigars, then insured them against, among other things, fire. Within a month, having smoked his entire stockpile of these pricey cigars and without yet having made his first payment on the policy, the lawyer filed a claim against the insurance company. In his claim, the lawyer stated the cigars were lost "in a series of small fires."

The insurance company refused to pay, citing the obvious reason, that the man had consumed the cigars in the normal fashion. The lawyer sued...and won!

Delivering the ruling, the judge agreed with the insurance company that the claim was frivolous. The judge stated that, nevertheless, the lawyer held a policy from the company in which it had warranted that the cigars were insurable and also guaranteed that it would insure them against fire, without defining what is considered to be "unacceptable fire," and thus was obligated to pay the claim.

Rather than endure a lengthy and costly appeal process, the insurance company accepted the ruling and paid $15,000 to the lawyer for the cigars lost in the "fires."

After the lawyer cashed the check, the insurance company had him arrested on 24 counts of arson! With his own insurance claim and testimony from the previous case being used against him, the lawyer was convicted of intentionally burning his insured property and was sentenced to 24 months in jail and a $24,000 fine.

Mr. Goldman must have had this same *creative consequences* thought as he sued for the rights to O.J's book, intending to market it with only one change—the title. "If I Did It," to "Confessions of a Double Murder."

Popcorn, Monopoly and wealth redistribution

Red states, blue states and political rhetoric are thrown at you from every ad, newspaper, and infomercial you happen to see. This year, through all that commotion a common phrase keeps reappearing, "wealth redistribution."

While this is one policy I wasn't excited about, I hadn't given any real thought to how it would affect me—until last Saturday night. My little sister was down from college for the weekend and we had decided to break out Monopoly.

Before we could begin the game, we'd prepared a big bowl of popcorn drizzled with butter, a bowl of apple slices and caramel dip and of course hot cocoa and marshmallows. Once in our pajamas, we were ready to settle in for a relaxing evening of buying, shouting, trading and making trips to the jailhouse—a perfect Saturday night.

Several hours into the game, a clear separation of wealth was becoming apparent. Multiple hotel chains were rapidly replacing the house conglomerate—on one side of the board. There was not a house in sight on the other side—nor any hope of building any time soon. The owner to those barren properties sat grim faced on my kitchen chair holding a stack of $1 bills and looking forlornly at the mortgaged side of all their titles.

Suddenly my sister piped up, "This isn't fair. The president says to redistribute the wealth. Spread it around a little bit." With that, she scooped the groups of houses off of Marvin Gardens and put one house each on Connecticut Avenue, Vermont Avenue, Oriental Avenue and Charles Place.

In that second, as I watched my hard-earned houses being "shared," I gained a whole new insight into just how much I disliked the proposed redistribution of wealth plan... what fun is work or Monopoly without a little old-fashioned American capitalism?

Freedom and pink sheets

I ran into town to get new sheets for my bed. Upon arriving at the store, I headed back to the bedroom section. There was only one style to choose from—and it wasn't bad—if you wanted striped, salmon pink sheets. They had pillowcases, shams, bed ruffles and sheets in every size—but only in salmon pink. There wasn't a white sheet to be seen.

I could only imagine what my husband would say about sleeping on salmon pink sheets—so I tried another store. Imagine my shock to see the exact sheet sets in the second store. Not another color or floral pattern on the shelves. I finally found a salesperson and asked if they had any other colors in the back.

"No," she said. "Martha Stewart decided that this type and color of sheet is better than your old sheets. It exfoliates your skin while you sleep as well as providing a soothing color for a deeper more relaxing night's rest. These sheets will also increase personal productivity so much that selling any other sheets has been banned and by 2014 every American will be required to buy these sheets not only for their own use—but also for their guest beds."

Fictitious and contrived you say? Perhaps. But no less frightening. We wouldn't want someone mandating a certain bed or color of car—yet with every right that is taken away from us, we come one step closer to salmon pink sheets.

While we're busy watching TV, our freedoms have been slowly ebbing away. We accept it because each bill has just enough sugar to help the medicine go down. No smoking in restaurants seems like a great idea (especially for non-smokers such as myself), but shouldn't it be the restaurant owner's decision—not the governments—whether to allow smoking or not? And while seatbelts may save lives—does the government really have the right to make it a law? Maybe they should outlaw eating utensils. After all wouldn't it be safer to eat with our hands?

What happened to personal choice, freedom and responsibility for our own actions? When a democracy can require every person to buy a product—any product—for our own safety and well-being…salmon pink sheets aren't far away.

Common sense? Where?

*C*ommon sense is a misnomer. It should instead be called extraordinary judgment reserved for a select group of rational people—their motto could be "the few, the proud, the ones with horse sense."

Earlier this summer, during a morning thunderstorm, my dog ran away. Several hours later I got a phone call from the Humane Society reporting that she had been found. I was delighted and erroneously assumed I could just go pick her up. They soon had me jumping through a series of hoops that kept me running between the police station, city hall, and the pound. The problem had nothing to do with the dog. There was a discrepancy in their paperwork and they didn't know who I should pay the fine to: the police station or the Humane Society. I offered to write a check and let them fill in the recipient when they figured it out so I could get back to work, or to write a check to each of them. They declined. It took four hours to get my dog back. When did paperwork become a substitute for service? What happened to our society? When did rules become more important than principles?

A while back my dad was waiting in line at the DMV, when his number came up the lady attendant was one of his old girlfriends from high school. They reminisced about old times while he filled out the required paperwork. When he realized he'd forgot picture ID, she handed him his forms back saying "without ID I can't be sure of who you are." Since when did a photo on a piece of plastic carry more clout than having known someone half your life?

This week, my husband stopped at a local fast food restaurant for lunch and discovered a large ice water was nearly as much as a large soda. "Since when did they start charging so much for ice water?" he questioned. "Well," the man replied, "you have to buy the cup and straw. But if you like, you can have a small ice water for free."

"Okay," my husband joked, "I'd like 15 free small ice waters."

Pulling around to the window, he was surprised and a little embarrassed when the man, without a trace of humor, handed him 3 cardboard drink containers filled with 15 small cups of ice water, along with straws. Did he ever stop to think that those 15 cups, straws, and carriers probably cost quite a bit more money than the one large cup? Judging from his expression—I doubt it.

Common sense left when people decided that salmon were more important than people, spotted owls more important than jobs, and body screenings at airports make you safe. I bet if we would stop and analyze many of our government policies, we might find they, too, are charging for a large water while giving out 15 free ones complete with straws and drink holder—and maybe, if you're not a citizen, they'll throw in the whole meal deal.

Who's on First?

*S*itting around a board game one evening, my sister missed a name, and questioned, "who?"

"Who's on first," someone piped up.

"I don't know," someone else answered. Which of course was followed by "third base..."

Then my dad questioned. "I just want to know who's Home?"

Without missing a beat, my husband shouted, "nobody!!"

We all laughed, but no one was smiling a few weeks later when we really started to wonder if nobody was home. Our annual family/friend vacation to the sand dunes had an abrupt change of plans due to the government shutdown.

Our campsite that we'd had reserved months in advance was closed "due to lack of government funding" according to the sign. Oddly though, the campground hosts were volunteers, and advance payment was required for our reservations. After a little scrambling and a lot of frustration later, we did find a great campground and were still able to make a good vacation out of it. I saw a sign that I had to include in our vacation scrapbook which had a picture of Smokey the Bear pointing his finger and saying "Only you can prevent forest fires...no really, I've been furloughed."

Amusing, but it did make me wonder what is going on in Washington. Closing memorials and hiring security to keep people out; closing down national parks and barricading them to prevent viewing?

I don't claim to be politically minded—but it sure seems that if you can pay government workers to close something down or keep people out, you could pay them to keep it open. Business 101 tells you cutting places that generate revenue is absurd.

Make cuts, but cutting things like national parks, Social Security and education, is like worrying about a skinned knee when the an artery is severed and gushing blood. We could start by cutting the government's credit cards.

You can't farm forever on credit lines—sooner or later you have to sell the crop and pay your creditors back. If the year was bad, you don't tell the cultivator you can't afford new shanks, and then turn around and buy the operator a new tractor. It's time to focus on the artery—not the skinned knee.

This is more than voting red or blue, this is about the Red, White and Blue. The government is supposed to belong to us. And right now it's floundering. I don't care if we vote against each other, worship differently, or have opposing beliefs about GMOs. I'd like to believe that "we the people" will come together to defend our precious country and constitution so we can all live the American Dream... before a dream is all that's left...and nobody really is home.

Traveling

I'd rather be lost in the woods,
than found in the city.

Here's your sign

*W*hat are people thinking? Have you ever seen the BUMP or DIP road signs? You're driving down the road, straining to read the yellow road sign, and just as you make out the words—your head crashes into the sunroof. I've often wondered if it wouldn't have been cheaper to just fix the bump or dip.

After hitting the dip, I begin rubbing the bump now on my head and thinking about many other strange, odd, and sometimes pointless signs that I've seen.

Driving back from California recently, I noticed a new road sign in Weed. The original sign had read "Weed Right–College Left." Which direction will your life go? The sign was stolen so many times the California Department of Transportation replaced it with "City Center Right—College of the Siskiyous Left." Not nearly so concise in my opinion.

A little less life-changing, but still head-scratching was a sign my sister and I discovered in Disneyland during a family vacation. While standing next to a sidewalk full of signs telling Disneylanders where to park strollers and store backpacks, we noticed a smaller green sign with white lettering: "THIS IS A BLANK SIGN! Please do not pay attention to anything you may see on this sign. We only wanted to let you know that this is a blank sign. With nothing on it. Except this message." With posters like this, it is little wonder why drivers often "pay no attention" to little white signs with big black numbers, all under the words speed.

The Bill Engvall lyrics described my favorite-to-date sign. "[Some people] should have to wear signs that just say 'I'm stupid.' That way you wouldn't…ask them anything. It would be like, 'Excuse me…oops, never mind, I didn't see your sign'."

Just last week, while driving the semi home from Portland my husband made our usual bathroom/snack stop at the truck stop in Biggs. As he pulled off the Interstate, he saw a man sitting on the corner holding a cardboard sign. He was about to look away, when he noticed the man's destination. In big letters the man had written "BIGGS."

I had just one thought: here's your sign.

It ain't what it used to be

I dread tax season. When it comes to the amount of money one spends, vague generalities somehow seem more palatable than seeing the exact figures. Especially when it comes to the fuel category.

I was recently complaining about the spike in oil prices to a non-farming friend. He agreed, adding his two cents. "I paid nearly $1,500 last year in fuel," he exclaimed, "with prices like that, I can't afford to drive anymore." At $1,300 just to fill the tank on the semi-truck, I wanted to smack him. I'd trade fuel bills with him any month—as I'm sure would every farmer, rancher or trucker.

Just four years ago, my dad and I road-tripped out to the Midwest. We were running low on fuel and had stopped at several stations, only to discover they didn't offer diesel. At this little wide spot in the road, we finally found diesel—at an exorbitant price. Bust as it was the only place for miles, necessity forced us to pay a whopping $1.50 a gallon! It was so outrageous, that we didn't "fill-er-up," and while my dad was pumping the fuel, I had to take pictures of the sign—for fear no one would believe we had ever paid so much for diesel! I'm glad I did too, for at this rate, my children will never believe we paid $1.50 either!

Gone are the days of "putting a couple of bucks in" and expecting to get anywhere. But of ever greater concern is the effect it's going to have on our farm commodities. When a tractor drinks 7 gallons of diesel an hour, it won't be long before the grower has more into the crop than the consumer is willing to pay. Guess it's time to either plant a bigger garden, find that unclaimed lotto ticket in grandma's purse, or see if Jed Clampett has any more swampland.

Accommodations for the adventurous

*T*raveling is always an adventure, and this trip was no different. I started putting on my shoes as we pulled into this hotel. My bones ached from traveling and it only took minutes to changes into swimsuits, grab towels and head for the bubbling jets of a much-longed-for jacuzzi.

Imagine my disappointment when we opened the pool house door to find...only a pool. The place was deserted, and it seemed wrong to go back to our room with dry swimsuits, so my husband and I tip-toed into the chilly water. Attempting to warm up, I began swimming laps. Side stroke first, then the back stroke.

I had just finished my first lap, when I glanced over to see a frog swimming contentedly about two feet away! I practically walked on water to get out of his way...I don't mind swimming with creatures in a pond...but an indoor pool? And besides, swimming side by side, his breast stroke made mine look like I was leaping Lilly pads.

But collecting wonderful horror stories of hotels is part of the traveling adventure. When I was younger, my family was vacationing in California. After driving for hours looking for a KOA campground, my parents finally stopped at a wide spot in the road that boasted two motels—both could have been stunt doubles for the Bates Motel.

My parents finally decided the Bun Boy looked safer. The bathroom's light was red. The thermostat was mounted upside down, there was a dead roach behind the chair, and the TV remote's off button had been removed. My mom wouldn't allow us to take off our socks...what a great adventure!

A few years later, I ended up back in that same little wide spot quite by accident. It was nearly 2 in the morning and once again exhaustion won out and we decided to spend the night.

Since my last experience in the town was so vivid, we chose the "other" motel. It didn't' have any roaches, but the carpet was covered in hair, the soap in the bathroom had been used, and the TV was bolted to the floor. We slept in our shoes and covered the pillowcases with T-shirts before we laid on them.

But nothing will compare to a bed and breakfast we stayed at in Canada. Breakfast had hair in it and the bed was a brass monstrosity on rollers...on a waxed hardwood floor! And did I mention it was our honeymoon?

The moral? Sleep is overrated—sometimes it's best to pass up a hotel for a really strong cup of coffee!

Cow tipping & the Power Pee

*G*rowing up in rural Oregon, there seemed to be no shortage of activities to fill Saturday nights: cow-tipping, rat stomping, and sending people snipe hunting. But every once in a while it was fun to venture out of Kansas and enjoy the sights and sounds of the big city.

One of my favorite venues has always been Disneyland: the rides, the magic and of course the cotton candy. On our first trip to the newly opened California Adventure my sister and I were enjoying the California Screamin' roller coaster, riding it three times back to back. On our way back for a fourth time our youngest siblings shanghaied us, and dragged us to the Maliboomer.

The Maliboomer is a 200 foot-structure designed to rocket you 180 feet in 4 seconds, before letting you free fall down. Then just before you reach the ground, it's back up to the top. This lasts for a very lengthy 45 seconds. A posted sign advises that this "herky jerky ride" is not recommended for anyone with neck or back trouble, heart problems, or expectant mothers. An oversight committee should add "weak bladders."

Our younger siblings clung tight to our arms preventing us from running, and before we knew it, we were locked firmly into our seats by big, black shoulder harnesses. A minute later, with shaky knees and slightly less-full bladders, my sister and I were kissing the ground, thankful to be alive. We agreed the Maliboomer was a misnomer, and subsequently dubbed it the "Power Pee."

Upon a bit of thought, we agreed that while Oz may be a bundle of lights and activities, there's no place like home. Rat stomping at home is every bit as enjoyable: your feet never have to go more than 20 inches off the ground and weak bladders are of no concern.

No Room at the Inn
for Mary, Julia Roberts or Benjamin Franklin

I was really starting to empathize with Mary and Joseph. We were at our third hotel, and still no room for us at the inn. The temperature was 4 degrees, my belly was hurting, I was pretty nauseated from the drive, and my head was really starting to throb. All I wanted was a place to lay down and a hot shower. But between no vacancies and no pets, we were striking out.

Arriving at our fourth hotel for the evening, there was a little sticker on the door reading "dog friendly." and there weren't many cars in the parking lot. I was beginning to feel hopeful. Ten minutes later we were pulling out of the parking lot looking for hotel number five. There was vacancy. They allowed pets. They wouldn't take cash! The magnetic strip on our credit card wouldn't scan in their machine and they wouldn't accept green legal tender.

I went from feeling like the virgin Mary to Julia Roberts in Pretty Woman—well except for the whole prostitute thing. She's on Rodeo Drive, and has wads of cash, but no one will sell her a dress. That's what I kept thinking about as we went from hotel to hotel—with no one willing to accept a green dollar. I can understand out of town checks...but cash?

An hour and a half after our first hotel stop we finally

found a hotel that would accept cash, but we had to pay an extra non-refundable $40 for the privilege of not using plastic.

The way the clerks looked at us, one would have thought we were trying to use salt blocks or cocoa beans to pay for a hotel room—not cold (literally frozen at 4 degrees) cash. Imagine Benjamin Franklin as worthless wampum. Makes me wonder if Mary and Joseph would have had better luck if they'd been carrying plastic?

A journey of a thousand miles begins with a cash advance

*L*ife and love are just two of the many lessons taught by traveling. I know of no better way to determine if you love someone or hate them than to travel with them. I'm not sure if it's the long car ride, or maybe reading the map wrong, getting lost, having flat tires, losing fan belts, spending the night in the Les Schwab parking lot, or driving on icy roads—but whatever it is, traveling seems to magnify all human emotions. I weeded out many boyfriends using this litmus test.

My husband and I love traveling, (sometimes even together), and recently made two road trips across the United States. The last one began on the eve of our 6-year anniversary. In keeping with tradition, we stopped at a truck stop and split a bean burrito—talk about romance.

But we figure that romance is less about the gift, and more about the manner of delivery. Same with traveling: it's about making the journey as enjoyable as the destination. A good traveler has no fixed plans.

Traveling also teaches the power of suggestion. Have you

noticed just how powerful those blue rest area signs are? You drive by the first one reading "rest area 5 miles" with a quiet, contented bladder. You pass the second, "rest area 1/2 mile" feeling a slight discomfort. By now you are debating whether or not to stop—when just 5 miles ago you were fine. Your tight schedule finally wins out, and you keep your foot on the accelerator as you pass the rest area. That's when you notice the smaller plaque under the blue sign: next rest area 130 miles. Suddenly your bladder is screaming, and you're out in the middle of nowhere—not a gas station, truck stop or tumbleweed in sight. The power of the blue sign.

I love all the little things that traveling teaches us. Like toleration; because inevitably, one person will have a bladder the size of a pea, while the other the size of a pumpkin. Through travel I've learned about priority packing: I lay out all the clothes I want to take—then take half the clothes and twice the money. Travel teaches patience: because no matter how fast you eat your continental breakfast, you can't leave until your companion is packed and ready to go. These lessons are half of the joy of traveling—the other half is watching your companion experience them!

Elvis who?

*T*aking the farm boy out of the country is like stretching a rubber band. It can be done, but sooner or later it'll snap back and you best be out of the way! One of our recent trips found us sitting in a hotel in Memphis, travel brochures spread out around us, deciding on the next morning's activity. We'd narrowed it down to two choices: a river boat tour of the Mississippi River or Graceland. Time to put it to a vote: my husband, voted for the boat ride, I voted for Elvis, and as Our Little One doesn't talk yet—he votes with me. That made 1¼ for me—and I began programming 3734 Elvis Presley Boulevard into Esmeralda (the GPS).

Before long we were standing in the Jungle Room, looking at his many gold and platinum records, walking through his private jet, and getting our pictures taken in front of his pink Cadillac. I was still in the midst of euphoria from getting to see the pink caddy in real life, when our Little One started waving delightedly and my husband picked up his snail pace. I shoved my camera away and hurried to keep up with them. I should have known. In a museum filled with Harley Davidsons, Stutz Blackhawks, a 1975 Ferrari, and several museums, my boys had found the one and only 4010 John Deere tractor. It was nearly impossible to pry the Little

One away, so I finished perusing the cars alone.

It wasn't until the next day when I learned just how excited my husband had been about seeing the King of Rock and Roll's home. We had stopped to visit some relatives in Oklahoma; my husband was chatting with my cousin and I was talking with his wife. Suddenly, he leans over to me. "What was the name of the place we were yesterday?" he asked, "you know, the dead singer?" No wonder he'd voted for the boat ride! Guess he has a long way to go before being "all shook up!"

Country mouse

$\mathcal{A}$s a child, one of my most prized possessions was a small Mickey Mouse record player. I spent hours beside it, coloring while it entertained me one side at a time with fairy tales and songs. I enjoy music a lot, but there is something about losing oneself in a carefully crafted story and I would listen to them over and over. It didn't matter that I knew the ending, the journey of the story always seemed to hold something new for me—and recently, on a trip to Michigan, I found another gem in a favorite story.

My husband likes to eBuy, and January found us packing our bags for a trip across the U.S. to pick up another piece of farm machinery. I was pretty excited by our destination, for it put us within hours of a college friend I hadn't seen for 7 years. She and her family live just outside Detroit; so at our request, her husband drove us into the city for a little sight-seeing. I didn't know much about the recent state of affairs, other than there were a lot of buildings that were boarded up.

I got my first wake-up call, when my friend's daughter spotted a firebomb just lighting up the afternoon sky. My friend said as it was "only a few hours 'til dark" it wouldn't be safe to exit off the freeway, "especially since we have kids with us."

I was too nervous to take out my camera to photograph the tall buildings without a single pane of glass; churches with blackened steeples and holes in the walls; nice looking rows of townhouses with every 3rd or 4th house graffitied and missing doors, windows and/or the roof. Perhaps they need to print more anti-gun zone posters—or maybe those anti-gun groups should go door-to-door and hand out tracts? (It might actually be helpful—it would either eliminate the guns or the groups).

The drive back to our friend's house was silent. My husband and I both trying to accept that the sights we saw were in the United States and not some blown-up third world country—or a Hollywood set for an end-of-the-world film.

Unlocking their front door, our friends assured us that their street was safe—it wasn't until you got another 6 or so streets down that you started running the risk of daily car-jackings—but that didn't stop them from having a gun in nearly every room of the house. That night, we laid on a deflating air-mattress and listened to fairly regular gunshots—and my mind drifted off to a long ago fable of the City Mouse and the Country Mouse. Never had I so fully understood the moral as that night. For it is indeed better to eat a pittance in peace, than a banquet in fear.

The tortoise & the hare: road trip

"The best laid plans of mice and men" should be my theme song. I wrote my whole week on the calendar in pen, which was my first mistake—farmers wives should never use pens except to sign checks and hold up their hair. My penned-in plans included accompanying my sister to a play on Friday; hosting a church youth party Saturday; and shearing sheep on Sunday. But while I was busy making plans—my dad and my husband were discovering online farm auctions.

Wednesday evening rolled around, and I was still blissfully ignorant of the coming change in plans. I didn't even know a cultivator had been purchased until 7:30 p.m. but by 10 p.m. I knew it was time to start canceling plans. By noon the next day, my mom, my 4-year-old and I, were pulling out of the driveway headed for Nebraska. We were hauling down a pickup and going to bring back a cultivator.

1,400 miles, 5 states and 26 hours later we were unloaded, reloaded, strapped, and refueled. My son had never been through the Dakotas before, so we'd decided to add some adventure to our trip and see some of the sights. We spent Saturday touring some of the caves (redneck style with a big load of farm machinery), drove through some of the wildlife parks and hit Mount Rushmore for photos. After snapping my last picture of the four presidents, we pointed the pickup toward home—and it was at that moment that I realized my mom and I have very different traveling philosophies.

My mom approaches traveling like she does anything else: get in, get the job done, and go home—no reason to dilly dally along. I, on the other hand, like to gawk, read the historical markers and take pictures of every last fencepost. It was like pairing the tortoise and the hare as partners in a race.

By midnight, I was slowing down for blowing weeds and dodging moving shadows. I was ready to find a hotel with a hot tub. My mom however, seemed bright-eyed and bushy-tailed and saw no reason not to continue driving the remaining 10 hours home. I couldn't understand her not wanting to stretch out and sleep horizontally—and she couldn't understand why I couldn't just lean the seat back and sleep for free. I later suggested that she should apply for long-distance cattle hauling. She'd be perfect—she'd drive straight through and wouldn't let things like sleep and food slow her down—she just laughed.

I'm not sure that my mother Hare will ever want to road trip with her daughter Tortoise again. Me and my tortoise shell like napping in the sun too much—and even when we are awake and underway we almost need slow-moving signs. But all in all, we had a good time...and thanks to my mom, we made great time. Arriving home early Sunday afternoon—just after the sheep shearer had finished up. Which concluded my list of "penned-in" calendar events. So I'm throwing away my pens and calendar, from now on I will try to expect the best, plan on the worst, and prepare to be surprised by all of it!

Cruise ship dieting

I travel a lot; I seem to hate having my life disrupted by routine. That may account for the 45,000 miles on my 15-month-old pickup. The mode doesn't seem to matter; it can be by air, by land, and most recently by sea.

My family and I recently took a cruise through some of the Caribbean islands. We had heard about all that great cruise ship food, and decided to try it out for ourselves.

They say the way to a man's heart is through his stomach, and upon discovering the 24-hour buffet, my husband was in love. Those who say you can't take it with you, never saw cruise ship passengers loading up their plates before heading back to their staterooms! In all honestly though, I must say we both loved it….a little too much. We boarded the ship as passengers and we left as cargo.

We had a splendid time, and all too soon we were waving goodbye to our newly made friends, exchanging numbers and promises of keeping up. As I went to put those numbers in my suddenly snug pants pockets, I learned a truth about myself: I am a nutritional overachiever.

Upon arriving home, I saw the damage those beautiful meals had caused. It created a fissure between me and the bathroom scales. We've never been close, but we've never been enemies before; so I went about repairing the rift in our friendship. I filled the fridge with lots of lettuce and veggies, I swapped out soda pop for V8 juice, and for desserts we began to eat dried fruit.

I dusted off my workout videos, got out my stair stepper, and even took my Pilates ring out in the tractor with me. I was determined this wouldn't take long. At the end of the first week, I stepped on the scales with anticipation....I had gained 1.2 pounds! This was not the way I had envisioned fixing our relationship, I shouldn't be doing all the work, shouldn't the scales have at least met me half way?

The second week I worked even harder, we went snow-shoeing until I couldn't feel my legs, I hit 4,000 on my stair stepper each day, and I started jogging. Then the moment of truth. I stepped on the scales...another half pound.

I've now been on a diet for three weeks, and the only thing I've lost is 21 days! It took awhile, but I realized not all relationships are worth fixing. The scales was "re-homed" to under the sink, next to the toilet brush.

Who's to say if those 10 pounds I'm trying to use are the ones that contain my humanity, my love, my genius? If 40 is the new 30, I think 140 should be the new 130!

And while I may be embracing my newly found "char-acter," I still will be working on a balanced diet: that's why you'll never see me with a bag of chips in only one hand. I've banished the scales, I'll just buy bigger jeans. So what if we left the ship as cargo, cargo still gets to travel!

Holidays

FAMILY

They drive you Crazy
They drive you Nuts
They drive you Loony

BUT

They Drive You.

Chocolate eggs & 'T' sticks

*T*oilet bowl cleaner, masks, urine remover, scrubber brushes, air fresheners and a toilet plunger were all carefully arranged in a bright orange basket. Sound like something on a hotel cleaning cart? Nope....it's an Easter basket. Chocolate bunnies and malt balls are for the novice—when it comes to Easter, my family is hard core.

While the cleaning items in the basket are useful...their real purpose was to disguise the focal gift in the basket...the "T" stick...

During a recent housecleaning venture, my cousin was mucking out the bathroom of a woman who must remain unnamed. My cousin brought in a dumpster and was hauling out loads of junk. This unnamed woman wasn't the most tidy woman in the world, and like so many women had an eclectic assortment of random junk. My cousin had finally worked his way into the bathroom and was filling up another box of garbage.

Cleaning around the toilet he found a dirty, old, metal rod with a narrow crook at one end. He picked it up and was just about to set it on the garbage box when our unnamed lady came bustling through the bathroom door.

"Don't throw that away," she hollered, noticing her rod

was heading for the garbage box. "It's not junk...that's my turd stick...it helps break up..." My cousin's brain blocked out the rest of her words. He looked down and saw his fingers still on the crook end of the rod—he could almost see bacteria begin to grow around his nails. "What about...?" he stammered, his bacteria-growing hand pointing to the toilet plunger.

"Oh, that comes next," our unnamed woman sing-songed.

Hours later, my cousin was still scrubbing his hands: dish soap, antibacterial soap, laundry soap, bleach, cleanser—and still didn't feel clean enough to touch his supper.

But as misery always has, and will continue to love company, he couldn't let that memory die alone in his own mind...and because of that, we have our very own "T" stick "that," my cousin delightedly informed us, "was authentically shaped." Carrying that orange bathroom basket home, I'm beginning to have second thoughts about chocolate bunnies and malted eggs.

Scientific Valentines

*V*alentines day is here once again, bringing with it chocolates, roses—and unmet expectations of romance. A day that men pretend to lose their wallets, and women pine over bouquets of over-priced roses; a day looked forward to by couples and dreaded by single people.

Now, however, singles have more chances than ever to find "that special someone." If traditional dating has yielded no results, one can always turn to science to find your "chemical match." For the amazingly low price of only $1,900, you can swab your cheeks for a DNA sample for analysis. Researchers will test six of your alleles to determine who your scientific other half is. Not as fun as dinner...but supposedly much more efficient in determining compatibility.

I didn't swab to check our compatibility...I scooped—dirt that is. We met while driving backhoes to trench an irrigation line. My compatibility checklist went like this:

-can work as hard as me. Check
-can solve problems I've created. Check
-can fix machinery I've broke. Check
- can back-fill holes I've dug too big. Check
-has his own tractor and jumper cables. Check

The wedding bells sounded, and we took that $1,900 we

"saved" on testing and honeymooned.

I wonder if what attracts people to gimmicks like this is the idea that a "perfect match" will mean a perfect relationship—one without the usual ups and downs they have experienced before? But a marriage without conflict is as ridiculous as a nation without crises.

I concede though, that a marriage made for scientific reasons is better than marrying for money...after all, you can borrow money cheaper.

Wisdom at Grandma's knee

*M*y grandmother has always been full of wit and wisdom, and usually has some amusing anecdote, rhyme or poem for nearly every occasion. Once she caught me smacking my gum and recited: "A gum chewing girl, and a cud chewing cow; what's the difference? Oh I see it now; the contented look on the face of the cow."

My grandmother collects poems as she goes through life, much like, she claims, a dog collects burrs as it runs through bramble. Recently a friend wore rubber boots and shorts over to help my grandparents do their chores. Which, she told him, reminded her of a poem. "The higher the mountain the cooler the breeze; the shorter the trousers, the cuter the knees."

I love traveling with her; she gives interesting, unusual or amusing tales on some of the most ordinary things. Memorial Day weekend this year was no exception. Camping at Lehmann Hot Springs we learned about sleeping habits.

Most of the older generation thought nothing about getting up at 4 a.m to begin their day...and most of the younger generation doesn't think much of it either! Early Sunday morning, while most of our group sat around a smoky campfire, one Sleeping Beauty hadn't budged from the back of my parent's toy-hauler.

As the sun hit 8 a.m. her significant other decided to wake her. The question was how. She was sleeping on hydraulic bunk beds, which begged consideration; and there were always the conventional methods like ice, water, taking her blankets, etc. Someone reminded him that she was sleeping in the back of a toy-hauler (which means the back wall of the trailer drops down making a ramp to load ATVs).

Rise and shine! The darkness was quickly replaced by bright sunshine streaming into her sleepy eyes. It wasn't the awakening kiss Sleeping Beauty enjoyed, and it seemed to throw off her entire day. Stumbling out of bed, she thought cocoa might clear her brain—and it probably would have—if she'd been awake enough to use hot water.

Later, I overhear her telling my grandmother about the episode (my grandma had also been sleeping and missed the incident). I had to smile; my grandma was in good form as she told Sleeping Beauty that she and my grandfather have always agreed that morning was the best time of the day... they just disagreed on where to spend it...adding yet another gem to my collection.

White elephants

I've heard people complain about Christmas being just an over-commercialized holiday, full of expense and waste—to those people I say, try a white elephant....

In Thailand, white elephants were historically regarded as holy beings, bringing fertility, prosperity, and power. They were given special foods and elaborate housing. It was forbidden to kill them or to use them for work. Therefore, the story goes, whenever the king wished to punish an obnoxious courtier, he'd make him a present of one of these pale pachyderms. It was a gift to be dreaded. Recipients could neither use the elephant nor get rid of it—and inevitably went broke trying to keep it fed.

Nowadays, the expression "white elephant" is used more generally to apply to any burdensome possession. Like the gold and green lamp Aunt Agatha painted. You wouldn't dare throw it out, but you also can't leave it anywhere that someone may see it! Gifts that are extremely tacky/ugly, and were given by a friend or close relative and can't be returned without potentially offending the giver, make the perfect white elephant. And while the game will invariably gain you a new tacky gift, it's much easier to throw out someone else's junk!

This year's items didn't disappoint. The laughter began

when Grandma Cleo just had to have the biggest box. It was a classic case of buyer's remorse as she took off the last of the wrapping, and she tried without avail to unburden herself. When she realized no one was sympathetic, she tried to seduce the giver into taking it back, as the 25-year-old VHS camcorder "might be very valuable on eBay." No one bought it...that night, or on eBay.

One gift that was sought after was originally opened by my dad. A surprisingly nice shower kit of Herbal Essence (some people are still new to the idea of giving junk). Unfortunately for him though, my Grandpa stole it, and in its place left a heavy box of torn, hardbound textbooks I'd found as road kill a few years earlier. Checking out the titles, he began muttering about the shampoo making my Grandpa's hair green, and the shower gel making him itch...don't worry Grandpa, I'm sure he was kidding?

My little sister scored big by opening a curious little machine. As her confusion mounted, so did my grandparents' laughter. They didn't know what it was either. Lacking instructions, or any other identifying marks, it wasn't useful to them, but being brand new, they couldn't just throw it out...a hang-up from the Depression, I think. But thanks to the white elephant party, they didn't have to. And who said Christmas had to be expensive?

There's only one rule to remember in playing with white elephants. After the gifts are opened, the elephants must all go home with their new owners. Elephant-sitting is not allowed in the United States!

Resolutions

*'T*is the season for New Year's resolutions: losing weight, spending more time with family, and climbing Mt. Everest.

Once the resolutions have been made, one will often set a time limit for the achievement, i.e., "I will lose 10 pounds by the end of January." Before the resolution has hardly been made, you begin to notice all those leftover Christmas baskets filled with cookies, divinity and lots of fudge. It would be wasteful to throw them out, and imagine the neighbor's hurt feelings if they discovered you feed their cookies to the dogs! That leaves only one option—you will just have to diet "extra hard" once the cookie platters have been emptied.

By now you're 3 pounds heavier than when you made your resolution—making it 3 times less likely you will achieve you January goal—which in turn makes it 3 times more difficult to even begin your diet.

The same scenario occurs when you try to spend more time with family. The sentiment is nice and probably sincere. But after a few visits with great aunt Hilda and her 50-year-old son that still lives at home—you are so fed up with family—they'll be lucky if you're ready to spend next Christmas with them!

Not only did the resolutions fail, they seemed to make the situation worse. You probably wouldn't have eaten all that fudge so quickly had you not been under a time schedule for your diet, which would have found you 3 pounds lighter. And if you hadn't spent all the time visiting Aunt Hilda early in the year, listening to her criticize every major decision in your life; you probably would have attended her birthday party in March—which would have certainly saved the family a huge brouhaha.

My conclusion is this: if you're going to make resolutions, be aware that you are most likely going to break them and the result may be exactly opposite of what you had anticipated.

So this year I passed up all the common resolutions in lieu of the following:

1. I will go back for seconds whenever the food is good (if the food is bad, seconds are optional).

2. I will spend less time apologizing for cat hair in my house (after all, I have cats—they have hair, and they perceive the furniture to be theirs).

3. Buy shoes when the mood strikes (and maybe even when it doesn't).

4. I will be satisfied climbing the stairs to work instead of Mt. Everest.

5. And though it will be difficult, I will give up changing handline every chance I get to go waterskiing.

While these resolutions may not find me skinnier, cleaner or more philanthropic, I figure in the long run they are healthier—while other people will begin to feel bad for breaking theirs, I will live the new year completely guilt-free!

Cheap family therapy

$\mathcal{E}$aster Sunday…a day when most people are donning their spring finery…and my family is preparing to go where no one has gone before…or at least since last Easter. It is the day of Grandpa Johnny's $50 egg hunt, and the family comes from distant states, often time spending triple that in fuel, for the chance at finding that revered egg. It is an egg that legends are made of, and stories are written about. The actual $50 matters less than holding the title as finder…the first family member to find it, still has the check in her bureau, and swears she'd have to be starving before she'd cash it.

The egg doesn't always get found, which only adds to the frenzied challenge. Past hiding places include being buried in the ground under some used tires; tied to an anchor and thrown into the feeder canal; half a plastic yellow egg, rolled up and stuffed inside a yellow wasp trap; and inside the heating coils of the water trough.

This is not an egg hunt for the faint or weak of heart. I've seen family members scour the dumpster and the feed bins, climb the barn roof and wiggle around under the foundation of the house. And we love it. This year, Easter fell on my little brother's 23rd birthday, and believing himself to be the master of his own destiny, decided he would find his own present...a $50 present.

We weren't but 30 minutes into the hunt, when my brother, who was kneeling next to the horse trailer started whooping and making loud but incoherent noises. He jumped into the air like a discharged bullet and vanished around the trailer still hollering like a banshee.

Of course the noise brought the family all running, and the look on Grandpa Johnny's face was somewhere between admiration and despair (he's not a big fan of giving out cash... note the locations of past $50 eggs). My brother was still hopping with a glow to rival any nuclear facility. While the rest of us had been tilling up the strawberry bed, and pushing big bales off the feed truck, he had been removing parts on the trailer. Which paid off, for he found the $50 egg inside the hubcap on the horse trailer....Happy Birthday to him!!

Later in the day I overheard one of the little girls telling her mom, "I like Easter better than Christmas!" And I had to agree with her. That $50 egg makes for cheap family therapy. The extended family all comes together, and we laugh and share while we dye the eggs; and push and shove while we find the eggs; and later we reminisce and tell egg tales (our family's version of fish tales).

We may not have the ruffliest family photos, but the egg hunt brings our family closer; it's like a spring renewal, and after all isn't that what Easter's all about?

Grandpa's legacy

"Your Grandma and I used to call those the family jewels," my grandpa said as his backless, sleeveless, legless, bottomless hospital gown gaped momentarily. In an ordinary family, the moment might have been a little awkward, but my family is anything but ordinary, which meant he kept talking about how valuable they were…which made the moment extraordinarily awkward and I think we were almost relieved when he began hallucinating about little red men, and chickens under the sheets. I had hoped the moment was forgotten, but as we were getting ready to leave, my grandpa had to give me a quiz to test my memory—and followed that up with, "I plan to read about this in your column next week." Ahhh...

Weeks passed, and I had nearly forgotten the instance, until Easter. Ordinary families dye eggs for the kids, hide eggs for the kids, and get Easter baskets for the kids. But we have already established that my family is far from ordinary. This year we dyed 15 dozen brown eggs and 2 dozen white eggs. And while the kids helped a little, it was the adults that were gluing hair to eggs and painting bikini bodies. We daubed, dipped, painted and waxed and even tried boiling some in silk ties…thus making real tie-dyed eggs.

Easter morning found nearly the entire extended family at my grandparents house, where we waited impatiently for the Egg Hunt Rules. This year our annual $50 egg had increased to $100, and we could hardly wait to grab shovels and ladders and begin hunting.

There were adults in trees, under the house, going through the garbage, and pawing through stacks of irrigation pipe. I saw adults going through wasp traps, sticking their hands in buckets of old grease and kicking over cow pies. All that work and no one did find the $100! (Or the $20, or the $5). After the hunt my Grandpa has to show us where the money eggs were hidden—just to keep him honest. The $100 was in a hole in the ground...under the right front tire of his feeding rig. The $20 was in a hole in the top of one of the trees. And the $5 was stuck in the middle of a section of wheel line.

Soon it was time for the Easter baskets. This year we had a canning basket (jars, dill, pickling salt, etc.), a relaxation basket (books, candles, coffee, etc), a greenhouse basket (sprayer, trays, fertilizer, etc.) a corn basket (corn meal, corn starch, whiskey, etc), and many other themed baskets.

I watched as people laughed at the surprises in their baskets. I love this holiday. I love dying the eggs, the baskets, the hunt...I love this crazy family. And suddenly I remembered the family jewels. Grandpa was right...they were valuable. Just look at the 3 generations of dirt-smeared, grease-stained kids and adults picking twigs out of their hair and dusting insulation off their jeans. Forget ordinary, this crazy family is extraordinary...thanks to Grandpa and his family jewels.

The Mother's Day myth

*H*ave you ever noticed how Mother's Day is spent in preparation for Father's Day? Somehow the fathers have convinced the mothers that what they want more than anything else is a day to work in the backyard, or maybe even the front yard.

A typical Mother's Day goes something like this:

Going out to eat.
(They take you to a restaurant for three reasons. 1. Most men don't enjoy cooking. 2. And even the ones that do, know that cleaning up after breakfast would be pretty difficult to get out of on Mother's Day. 3 Men know you must have a good breakfast if you are going to keep up your stamina throughout the day.)

Stopping at a lawn and garden center on your way home.
(This reason seems pretty obvious...but it's not quite as straightforward as you would think. If you look around at the couples and families in these stores, you'll notice that the mother is often with the children looking at trees or flowering shrubs...and there are groups of men stand-

ing around the barbecue section. More on this in a bit.)

Arriving home, anxious to plant your new purchases.

(The rest of the day is spent pulling weeds, cleaning flower beds, making raised beds, bringing in rock, putting down new bark, maybe even planting a tree or two. Here's where one really needs to be observant.

The mother is usually elated, and happily digging in the dirt or pulling weeds. The children's attention span waned as soon as the word weeds was mentioned.

And the father is hard at work deciding where the tree would best be planted...this usually takes a significant amount of time...after all, a tree is so permanent, one wouldn't want to plant it in a poor location.

The father usually figures out the perfect location about the time the last weed is pulled. Then the father plants the tree: either with a machine (which will always make him happy) or by hand when the rest of the family is around to see how hard he is working.

This has now completed the day.

The mother will feel quite pleased with all the hard work that has occurred, and be thankful for a special day just for her. The father will also feel quite pleased with all the work that has occurred, and be thankful he lucked out of weed patrol once again. The kids will just be thankful the day is over, and they won't have to pull weeds together for at least another year.

A typical father's day goes something like this:

A nice home-cooked breakfast.

Sometimes just for the father, sometimes for the father-in-laws too. The mother grocery shops the weekend before to make sure she has everything on hand. Then gets up extra early to have it all prepared. After breakfast, the guys gravitate outside to admire all the hard

199

work they've done on the landscaping recently—the new beds, the trees, the weed-free flower gardens....

Then comes the gifts.

Remember that time he spent looking at barbecues? He either picked out a new one, or found some new accessories to go with his current grill, and he's been dropping hints since Mother's Day.

The barbecue.

The fathers put on aprons, wield their utensils like kings holding scepters and begin making dinner...well, at least the barbecued portion. The mothers have already made the potato salad, and whatever fixings are to go along with it. The fathers stand at their post rubbing and flipping and impressing their children, until the mothers have set the table and put the drinks on ice.

Later that evening.

Everyone makes a fuss over what a great job the father has done on the barbecue, and he will feel pleased and satisfied. The mother will feel like she has married a great provider, and the kids will feel like they have the world's most awesome dad.

And somehow, we all believe it; and next year will be even better...because the lawn will look even nicer than this year...as there will be yet another tree or shrub or maybe even a new fence for Mother's Day!

Weather & Water

"The trouble with weather forecasting is that it's right too often for us to ignore it and wrong too often for us to rely on it."

~Patrick Young

The first day of spring

"You sure can tell it's spring," I said, gesturing toward the blue sky and the warmth it was exuding.

"Oh, I know," the lady at church responded, "and I haven't had time to replace my black nylons with white yet—I've got to get on that."

Smile and nod. That's my catchall expression when I've gotten into a conversation that's over my head. Smile and nod.

With the change in the weather, I hadn't even considered changing the color of my nylons. I thought as long as there were no holes they were wearable. I did change from insulated boots to cowboy boots though...I wonder if that counts for something?

Of course in the world of socialites and fashion, spring probably arrives under Easter bonnets and in new summer dresses.

While I may not be dressed for it, I am vividly aware of "the first day of spring." It doesn't really correspond with the calendar day of spring...but it's the real day. I never know from year to year exactly when it will happen, but when it does—I know. This year it occurred last Thursday. I was feeding our sheep, when I heard the words that call summer back from the grave of winter—"Brianna, I need your help laying out the sprinkler pipe..." Yup, the summer's waking up, I can already feel the sweat running down my neck and the mud slurping at my rubber boots.

Maybe when I'm old, I can hang up the sprinkler pipe for an Easter bonnet and the right color of nylons...but by that age I suppose I will only wear purple nylons anyway—to match my permed purple-tinted hair.

Water-witched?

*I*f I was to have a love affair, it would be with water. Friday afternoon rolled in hot and muggy and I had one thought: "river, river, river, river." While chatting with a girlfriend, I was delighted to hear that she was almost finished spreading out clumpy wind rows of hay.

I had one more field to rake and soon we were off. Nothing makes me happier on a hot day than a good ski at the river. We hooked up the boat, loaded the Jeep, and spent a couple of hours relaxing in the cool water of the Columbia.

Too soon dusk was upon us and we decided to head back. Only the boat had other ideas. It wouldn't move. We tried waving to the last remaining boat in the river, but they just kept going.

We tried the horn…it was broken. We tried the canned air horn in the jockey box…the button was corroded shut. We tried the cellphones…no reception. Finally decided to paddle…with water skis.

The current kept us moving, away from the boat dock, and we finally made it to shore about two miles away from the docks. Which put us back home close to 1 a.m.

Saturday came just as hot and muggy, and my girlfriend

and I decided we'd use their boat. Both our families came along, and after less than an hour, we were dead in the water. The same problem as my boat had.

Monday rolled around, clear, hot, and a bit breezy. While bemoaning the misfortune of my boat, a cousin offered to take me windsurfing instead. I was elated. I've always wanted to try that. Evening came, and we headed off. The river was glass. Not a hint of wind. We waited for several hours and never encountered a hint of breeze. No windsurfing for me.

Tuesday, still hot. I'm swathing, wishing I could find some water. I ran a sprinkler pipe through the header. Luckily it wasn't too bent. Second pass through the field turned up another pipe, only this time I fed the whole birdy and riser through the header. I was looking for water…not water pipes!

Wednesday. Hot, hot, hot. I took watermelons to the farmer's market...and left my water bottle at home. I was in the full sun, and did I mention it was hot? And not a drop of water at the market. I came home with a headache.

Thursday my sister and I were driving through town, pulled up at a stoplight, and suddenly the temperature gauge in my Jeep shot up, hitting red. Steam billowed out from under my hood, and an alarm bell went off. I pulled into the parking lot, shut my Jeep off and drifted to a stop.

My radiator hose had cracked, and sprayed out all the water. I wanted river water…not HOT water! While I was waiting for help to arrive, my little boy fell off a retaining wall giving himself an enormous goose egg and black eye.

It took 6 days for me to decide that my love affair won't go anywhere…you just can't trust water: even a straight stick turns crooked in it!

Three visitors

I received three unexpected visitors last week. Wednesday dawned hot and clear, a perfect time to knock down some alfalfa.

But first, as any wise farmer does, I checked the weather forecast. 0% Thursday, 10% Friday, and 0% through the following Friday. Those were odds I could live with, so I loaded up a bag of toys and snacks, and the Little One and I headed out.

I had just finished opening up the field when I received my first visitor. It was an old-timer waiting at the edge of my next pass. I didn't catch his name, but his first job made an impression. After realizing my husband wasn't home, we made quick small talk. While discussing my Little One waiting in the swather, he sighed, "Kids today, just got no ambition. Why, when I was 14, I was running moonshine between two counties!"

Still chuckling to myself, I climbed back into the swather and finished my field. I had barely driven the swather back into the yard, when visitor number 2 stopped in. "You sure you wanna cut hay today? I just heard on the radio it's s'posed to rain Saturday and Sunday?" I assured him I'd checked the forecast and it looked like great hay-drying weather for the next 10 days. His disbelief was apparent, and I pulled my laptop out and showed him the weather report. He scratched his chin, "Well in that case, I reckon I'll cut some of my own hay."

He went off to his swather and I climbed back in mine, and we both proceeded in knocking down several more fields of alfalfa.

And that's when visitor number 3 came—Rain. Rain is tenacious. Rain is devious. Rain sees a 0% chance written by some novice meteorologist and figures a lesson must be taught. Rain is also magnetically attracted to active swathers. Rainstorms will travel thousands of miles, against prevailing winds for the opportunity to rain on freshly cut hay. And the more hay that is down, the stronger the magnetic pull.

So next time the day is hot and clear, and the weather report says 0% precipitation, unexpected visitors might see me wearing galoshes and shuttling moonshine between two counties.

Dating & Marriage

Love is the thing that enables a woman to sing
(or at least not swear)
while she mops up the floor after her husband has walked
across it in his Muck boots.

Marriage and haircuts

*C*oming from a farming family, I knew when I said "I do" to a farmer that I was expected to do more than the dishes and my hair. A placard in our bathroom reads: WANTED! GOOD WOMAN. Must be able to clean, cook, sew, plant, and harvest crops. Must have John Deere tractor and barn. So it was no surprise to be eating breakfast, lunch and midnight snacks in a tractor seat.

My friends had always told me how there would be a lot of changes and surprises once we tied the knot: our conversations, our dates etc. They were right—kinda. Our long distance telephone conversations changed to CB banter in separate tractors.

Our date nights changed from baling hay for my dad—to putting up our own. And we still fall asleep during movies—it's just our own TV now, instead of my parents'.

But there was something that did come as a surprise to me. In addition to driving machinery, getting my pesticides license, paying the bills, feeding the animals, and learning how to correctly swing a bale hook—I now had to learn to cut hair.

Growing up with two sisters, I learned to cut, feather, layer and style—using scissors. But never once had I held a pair of clippers. That first haircut—uh—let's just say it's a good thing Les Schwab is generous with their hats. Thankfully, over time they have improved—his ears that is.

Last time though, I had a sudden thought: why was I expected to cut his hair—while I had to pay for a trim? Where was the equality in this relationship? Before I could think through the wisdom of this, I was the one on the kitchen bar stool. Looking in the mirror 10 minutes later, I was wondering why I care about equality. But my husband assured me, by tilting my head 45 degrees, my hair would look almost even. After another 15 minutes on the bar stool, my head was nearly back to center.

On our way to church the next morning, I figured he had done okay—all considering. I might even let him try it again sometime—I just wish my John Deere hat matched my high heels.

Boyfriends & ZIP codes

*N*o! No! No! No! I recently read that one-half of the troubles in this life can be traced to saying yes too quickly, and not saying no soon enough. That was how my two special guy friends came to know about each other in college.

My mother had always told us it was okay to have multiple boyfriends...as long as you kept them in different ZIP codes. What she forgot to mention, was sometimes you must say "no" to some of their dates or they just might meet each other!

Guy friend #1 and I had just come back from a pleasant weekend with friends at the coast. We had transferred all his stuff to his car, and if he would have just left for his study group like he'd planned, everything would have been great.

But he needed to use the bathroom, and then get a glass of water, and then he figured he may as well stay and eat dinner with us....

That's when the doorbell rang. Guy friend #2 had shown up on his bike to welcome us all back from our weekend getaway. The timing couldn't have been worse. There was so much testosterone in the air.

My roommate pinched me in the side as she ducked into her bedroom. Wimp!

Three hours of explaining later, I had zero special guy friends in no ZIP codes. And it took a couple of days and a lot of sweet-talking to remedy that situation.

And what did I take away from this situation? Learn to say No! It will be of more use to you than learning Latin. Although my husband had his own take on the situation...*may the best man win!*

Our first big fight

$\mathcal{D}$uring the library's annual book sale, I was skimming the tables looking for my choice authors. In between action/adventure and mystery, were the self-help books. I perused through them for no other reason than my eyes have been word deprived this harvest season. What I saw amazed me. There were countless books on how to survive the first year of marriage.

As I am nearing my third anniversary of married life, I was intrigued. A quick thumb-through highlighted chapters dedicated to fighting fair, communication, love languages, etc., things I would expect to find in a book on relationships. What I found interesting though, was the preface. Most indicated how difficult that first year was to endure, and if a couple could make it through the first year (thanks to their tips of course), the subsequent years would become easier.

Thinking back to that first year, I remember only one fight. We are two opinionated people, so there were many differing opinions on things, such as: cotton or flannel sheets, and who gets to drive the new tractor—but only one bona-fide fight. Getting ready for bed, I snuggled into the cotton sheets, right next to Sapphire, my Siamese cat. I have been sharing my pillow with Sapphire since I was 9, when I would leave my bedroom window open for him to sneak in.

Crawling under the covers, my husband started whining about how much room "that cat" took up. My feathers ruffled a little at "that cat," as Sapphire is more human than some people I've known. But as I fall asleep quickly, all would have soon been lost to dreams if my husband had not kept up the quiet muttering. As Sapphire swished his tail across the pillow in disgust at having to share his bed, my husband lost his cool. "That's enough! I'm tired of cat hair on my pillow. And I'm tired of having to sleep around that cat. Either he sleeps on the bed—or I do."

Sapphire smiled wickedly as he stretched across the now vacant pillow. But after establishing the pecking order, we've been realistically happy ever after...maybe I should write a self-help book.

September secrets

*S*eptember is a month for secrets. My little sister's birthday is the 2nd, my husband's is the 23rd, and mine is six days later. So sneaking around in whispers and telling secrets is naturally part of the fun.

Now I've been told that if you really want to keep a secret, you don't need any help...but what's the fun in that? It's always more fun to tell somebody else not to tell anyone! Such was the case with my birthday present this year. It was a Saturday afternoon, and we were enjoying that lazy after-church feeling. Legs kicked up on the couch, I was settling into my "lay-activities" when my husband bursts out "do you want to know what your birthday present is?"

I'm suddenly awake. Secrets in September are good—but it's still August—you can't find out your birthday present before your birth-month! Then again, he's got my curiosity up now. What could be so exciting he couldn't keep it a secret any longer? "I don't know," I asked, "do I?"

"Ya, ya, you do! You really do!" he bubbled. And then he shows me a picture of a Yamaha Raptor that he bought for our annual trip to the Oregon sand dunes. I'm thrilled. I've always wanted a non-tax-deductible four-wheeler, (the kind that doesn't come with a sprayer mounted on the back, or a tool box and sprinkler pipe fittings on the front).

I can already feel the crunch of the sand, and hear the spray of ocean water against my tires. Meanwhile, my husband is excitedly telling me all about the features, and then he added, "I wanted to have it shipped directly to the dunes, Really surprise you on your birthday."

"That would have been awesome," I agreed. "Why didn't you do it? Was the shipping too expensive?"

Suddenly his face turned solemn and his voice lowered. "I wanted to real bad. But I can only keep one secret at a time—and I figured you'd rather me keep the other one," he said, his eyes flickered to my belly. I smirked. We had decided to keep Junior a secret for 5 months.

I guess before I take my husband Christmas shopping, I'll have to ask if he's already keeping a secret...after all it's pretty obvious he can't keep two!

New baby shakes up gender roles

*T*here have been many changes in our house with the recent addition, and I don't mean just diaper changes. Bedtime has gone from 10 or 11 to 8ish (when the baby goes to sleep). Mornings have also changed, from 6ish to 7ish (for the baby and me anyway). But even more radical than the time changes are the household changes.

Our cats have become attention-deprived, and will perform all the tricks they know when guests arrive—in an attempt to get a little petting. And our house went from being pastor-visit-ready, to embarrassing even when my mother stops by.

My husband and I were talking about these changes, and how I wish he'd contribute more to the domestic chores. In recent years gender roles have definitely softened, but it is still more likely to see a woman in a business suit and briefcase, than it is to see a man with a duster and can of Pledge.

While I appreciate that my husband cooks, a new baby in the house has made me wish he cleaned toilets too.

Discussing this one evening, I commented that I thought my mom has scrubbed our toilet more than he has (she cleaned it once).

He looked appalled. "I imagine I've cleaned it at least 5 times." And you know, I had to admit he was right. Those 5 times were definitely imagined! Some things will never change no matter how lax the gender roles.

.com baby

*T*imes are changing. And sometimes I wonder how we are supposed to change with it. It's easy to change from wringer washers to front loaders and from black and white to HDTV. And I can't say I'm real sorry to say goodbye to visiting gloves and cloth diapers...but there are a few aspects of change that really are frightening... and I'm not talking about identity theft, phishing online accounts, and credit card debt.

As I watch my little toddler crawl into cupboards and bang on pots, I suddenly realize that change has put the stork on the endangered species list. I fear the day when my little boy will one day ask where he came from. In this, parents of yesteryear lucked out.

In today's age of technology, telling him the stork brought him will be akin to telling him I walked to school—10 miles—uphill both ways. He'll just pull out his phone, access the Internet, pull up the GPS coordinates of my hometown, discover it was only 6 miles, with less than a 0.2% grade one way—and then call me on walking to school at all.

I'm afraid "uphill/barefoot" stories and storks are quickly becoming a forgotten notion of a generation gone by. "Where did I come from?" stories will not start with K-I-S-S-I-N-G in trees; with love coming quickly and marriage preceding the baby carriage—which the stork brought tied up in pink or blue ribbons.

Today's kids are too Internet-savvy to buy it. The stork has become online dating...and soon Generation X'ers will be telling their kid that Mom and Dad got together in a chat room on Yahoo. Chatting turned to regular email and it all let up to a meeting in a cybercafé. They went into a private room and googled each other, then Mom downloaded from Dad's hard drive. Neither one had a firewall...but it was too late to hit the delete button. Nine months later a little pop-up appeared that said, "You've got Male!"

Wheat, strawberries, & a poem

*H*is forehead glistened in the last reddish rays of the hot July sun. The evening was warm, but not sweat-worthy. I had been enticed to Walla Walla with homemade ice cream and strawberry shortcake. After a delicious supper, we walked amicably down a little country road, enjoying the remainder of a sultry summer evening.

I had met my husband at the local community college. We got to know each other over many afternoons spent on a backhoe digging an irrigation system for the college. Our conversations had always been interesting and easy—but tonight there was the unmistakable taste of tension in the air. My attempts at lighthearted banter fell short. By the time we reached one of his wheat fields, we were walking in awkward silence.

The wheat stalks waved gently in the evening air. He'd said he was going to start combining soon. Just about that time, we came upon an unusual V shape that had already been combined. He gently touched my elbow to guide me off the road and into the 'V.' Which I discovered later was actually a 575 foot heart, filling nearly 16 acres.

I could feel my eyebrows squeezing together questioningly as he fumbled a dirty piece of notebook paper out of his pocket and started to read:

> *"Out in the middle of my wheat*
> *I stand beside a girl*
> *A girl I find so sweet*
> *More beautiful than any pearl.*
> *To her I must confess*
> *A relationship I'd like to start*
> *The answer I do hope is Yes*
> *From her I do not want to part*
> *And if she says no*
> *There must be a reason*
> *I will then go*
> *For now is not the right season."*

He then lowered the paper with trembling hands and made a quick swipe at the ever-growing sweat beads on his forehead. That was 10 years ago. And with each passing year we have discovered that celebrating an anniversary is more than just an excuse for a nice dinner. It's a celebration of love, trust, partnership, combine upgrades, tolerance and tenacity…not necessarily in that order—and not necessarily the same from year to year.

Love: before & after

Sitting in the fairground bleachers at Walla Walla's concert last year, my husband and I did a little people-watching during the intermission. We attempted to distinguish between the couples that were dating from the ones who had already tied the knot.

We didn't base this on wedding or engagement rings—but on the rest of their attire. For example, the unmarried men seemed to be wearing much more cologne than their married counterparts.

The two couples directly in front of us were decidedly not married. The night was quite chilly; I was dressed in jeans, sweater, boots, jacket and a scarf—and I wasn't exactly warm. The girls in front of us were both wearing short denim skirts; one had a spaghetti strap top, the other went strapless, and both wore little flippy sandals. The outfits would have been super cute if they hadn't accessorized with an immeasurable amount of goosebumps. And each time the wind shifted, we were assaulted with a ferocious amount of cologne from their two dates.

Directly to our right there was another couple—married we decided. He smelled normal, and she was dressed in jeans, boots, an oversize coat with an Eskimo fur hood and mittens—not exactly classy—but warm and snuggly. We continued our "married or just dating" game until the concert started again, but it got me thinking…marriage does change more than just an address.

Here's a few things that seem to change before and after falling in love.

Before—*She thinks my tractor's sexy.*
After—*But not jacked up in the yard.*

Before—*You take my breath away.*
After—*I feel like I'm suffocating.*

Before—*"I love the way you take control of the situation."*
After—*"You controlling, manipulative egomaniac…."*

Before—*Saturday Night Date Night.*
After—*Monday Night Football.*

Before—*"Momma, he's crazy—crazy over me."*
After—*Just plain crazy.*

Before—*$60/dozen.*
After—*$1.50/stem.*

Before—*Turbo-charged.*
After—*Jump-start.*

Before—*Shut up and kiss me.*
After—*Shut up.*

Before—*I can hardly believe we found each other.*
After—*I can't believe I ended up with someone like you!*

Forever my Deere

*M*y husband and I are quite partial to green: green grass, Green Acres, and of course green tractors. While we were dating we came up with a poster entitled "All I Need to Know about Life I Learned from My John Deere." It reads:

- *Deere can't outrun Pigs*
- *You can't jump puddles in your tractor*
- *Tires and cellular phones aren't compatible*
- *You don't need to dress up for a date when you have hundreds of acres to rake*
- *John Deere —don't leave home without one*
- *John Deere—where no other tractor has gone before*
- *The few, the bold, the John Deere*
- *Life marches to the beat of a diesel engine*
- *Bury your mistakes deeper than your plow shanks*
- *A letter describing a relationship break is a Dear John letter; a letter describing an equipment break is a Deere John letter: avoid both*
- *You can't judge a book by its cover—but a Ford painted green is no John Deere*

If our relationship over the years was a color—it would have been green. We met in the ag department of BMCC, and our relationship blossomed green over 4 tires and a loader (and a forklift thrown in for variety). We planned our wedding over CB's while baling hay late into the night. It was easy to understand then, why we picked 'forever my Deere,' as our wedding theme.

As the years came, so did our little boy—and what better way to welcome him into the world than a baby shower cake topped with green tractors. And much to some people's surprise we do let him play with other colored tractors. We figure it's like dating: you have to date a few wrong people to appreciate the right one. What better way to appreciate green than to play with red?

But in our green-filled life, we have found one buyer take note: there is one piece of equipment they won't stand behind...their manure spreader!

Broken gas cans

*I*f it ain't broke, don't fix it, seems so logical one would wonder why it even needs said. But it doesn't seem to be a commonly held theory anymore. A few years into our marriage, a well-meaning woman suggested we attend a local marriage counseling weekend.

I laughed because the psychologist teaching it had less than a year of marriage under his belt. I quickly realized my laughter was not well-received and she was indeed serious about our attendance.

I used the "if it ain't broke," proverb, to which she replied that marriage is not something that will thrive on its own, it must be tended and watered, (and I guess that included counseling). I agreed that marriage can't work without any attention, after all one can't expect a baler to work all season without adding twine and grease—maintenance is good. But any farmer worth his salt wouldn't mess with a properly functioning knotter!

Checking the oil and adding fuel isn't the same as splitting the tractor just to see why it's running properly. Why should a marriage be any different? The woman walked away with an exasperated "maybe one day you'll learn" expression on her face. My logic didn't seem too logical to her, and I'm starting to feel that she's not alone. I think the gas can legislature stands with her.

Anyone who's had to buy a gas can in the last 3 years knows what I'm talking about. No vents. Ever tried to fill up a tank from a non-vented can? You're trying to get the wheeline out of the way of the tractor, but first you have to fill the empty move tank. Gurgle, gurgle-spit, slosh, glug-glug-glug…5 minutes elapse, your arms start to ache, and gas keeps gurgling around the nozzle. The tractor is now waiting on you. You figure you've got at least a gallon in, so you quit pouring and start it—only to repeat this a day later when you're in a bigger hurry yet.

What was wrong with the old gas cans? They didn't bloat when they got hot, only to burp gasoline when opened. They also poured quickly and with ease. Why would the EPA "fix" something that worked so well.

The only benefit I can see from the cans working so inefficiently is this scenario: Wife runs out of fuel, calls husband to bring gas. Husband arrives with a 5-gallon gas can. Wife takes the fuel cap off and steps aside. Husband puts the nozzle up to the tank and while typically this would be the time for mentioning the Wife's forgetfulness to take the car to the fuel station, the slow 'glugging' instead causes him to rant about the idiocy of vent-free fuel cans… "if it ain't broke…. DON'T FIX IT!"

10 hot & steamy dates for farmers...

*W*e interrupt this marriage to bring you...farming season. Pick up any book on relationships and somewhere in there it will tell you how important it is to set aside one night a week for date night.

Obviously the writers were not farmers, or married to farmers. As any farmwife would attest, a date during harvest would not be a leisurely dinner and a romantic stroll in the park—holding hands and dreaming about the future. Instead it would be spent a) worrying about all the things you should be doing, b) on the phone attempting to talk an employee through a machinery break, c) inhaling dinner, so you can get back to work, or d) all of the above.

Recently a friend told me how important a weekly date was to maintaining a healthy marriage. At first I heartily disagreed. But after some serious thought, I recanted. It wasn't the dating I disagreed with—it was the format. A weekly date night during harvest? Not going to happen. But dating through the summer is possible—if you are a little creative with your definition of date.

I found a top 10 list of summer dates, and added my own brand of "romance" to them to make them easy to achieve—even for those of us who find dating between the months of March and October difficult.

10 dates, even the busiest of farmers can enjoy

10. Go shopping together…add some zap by holding hands while you head to the local Feed Store and pick out a new electric fence to keep in those pesky cows you've been chasing all morning.

9. Have a picnic…during wheat harvest, swing by the truck stop for some burritos and eat them on the way to the grain elevators.

8. Play a game…add a little friendly competition to your baling. See who can go the longest without breaking a shear bolt.

7. Learn something new together….try out a new farm implement together. Install a new GPS system together, or try out the telemetry on your center pivot.

6. When it gets hot, find water…and your irrigation boots, shovels, and maybe an excavator, as the two of you spend the afternoon cleaning ditch.

5. Go berry picking…this one's sure to spark a flame as you share a couple of blackberries together before you do your best to burn those pesky bushes off your fence rows.

4. Take a drive…through the John Deere dealership…try to keep the drool to a minimum…it's not nearly as romantic on the windows as steam.

3. Attend a food festival…this is really a great two-in-one date. Find the nearest Farm Fair where you can usually find some great foods, all the while earning your pesticide credits. It's better than dinner and a movie!

2. Wine Tasting…it's not so much wine as fermented Gatorade and old Mountain Dew, but you enjoy some great laughter as you "taste" and "swirl" whatever remains in the bottles behind the tractor seat.

You can discuss its "vigor" or "earthiness" (which is often caused by the ring of dust around the lid). This one is best done in the middle of the night, when you are already semi-drunk off sleep-deprivation.

1. Sweat together…I think the article was referring to a gym. But nothing spells sweat like changing handline on 6-hour sets. So move pipes, burn calories, raise endorphins and brag to your friends about your "hot and sweaty" dates with your sweetheart.

Animals & Pets

Don't corner anything you know to be meaner than you.

Pregnancy excitement

I recently received a letter from the senior class of a little island school in the Pacific. In the letter, the class wrote that I had been one of their most "beloved teachers," and they invited me to come back to speak at their graduation ceremony in the spring. I didn't know whether to scream, laugh, or cry...so I jumped up and down instead. I was so excited to think that I had actually made enough of an impression on these kids that 3 years later they would ask me to speak at their graduation.

Excitement was bubbling out of me and I had to tell someone. So I picked up the phone...and as so often happens when you NEED to talk to someone....I left a message on their voice mail, urging them to call back soon.

That's when excitement turned to shock. The first three friends to call back made this comment: "So...are you pregnant?" WHAT??

When you are dating, the common response to "guess what?" is: "are you getting married?" And now it has morphed from marriage to children!

And even if I did think bloating and maternity clothes sounded fun, I am afraid to have children as I think they would be part cat—let me explain....

I was over at a colleague's house recently, and he was demonstrating how talented his dog was. He would show her a stick, make her lay down, then throw the stick behind her. After a time he would tell her to fetch, and she would repeatedly whirl around and hunt for that particular stick until she found it. I was duly impressed.

My dog is too cat-like to fetch. She may bring back a stick once. But she sees no reason to retrieve something that I'm just going to throw again. She'll give me this "if you didn't want it—then why did I go get it?" expression. My dog is a cat with a wagging tail.

Although they both have four legs, the difference between cats and dogs is this: a dog sleeps on your bed because he loves you—a cat, because he loves your bed. Somehow my animals (dogs, sheep, cows) have all grown up cattish—and I'm afraid any children I have will be moody, independently cat-like...and meow!

So next time I have exciting news—I think I'll skip the voicemail—I don't want morning sickness.

Breezers rides the bull

"*Y*ou're up," my friend laughed while her eyes sparkled impishly, "it's your turn to ride the bull!" Never in my life have I pretended to be a cowgirl—a farm girl, yes—but a cowgirl? No. I used to ride horses when I was little—then my dad introduced me to motorized transportation: four-wheelers, motorcycles, scooters—things that never had to be coaxed or encouraged. When you were done riding them you just shut them off. There was no wiping down sweaty hair and cleaning tack. I still like the occasional horse ride—for a quarter at K-Mart.

In college I earned my nickname, Breezers, meaning "runs from cows." Most of the details escape me, I just remember standing in the corrals, when an old white, blind cow burst through a gate and comes running toward me. "Cut it off, cut if off," people were yelling at me. I took a good (but quick) look at the angry, blind, estrogen-loaded bovine running straight at me—1,200 pounds of mad cow—and I cleared a 6-foot fence without touching it—let some other idiot "cut her off."

I do like animals, as long as they're not significantly bigger than me—that's when my antiperspirant fails me. Unfortunately, being a farm girl also involves a pretty bad case of "anything boys can do, I can do better." And I'd just seen a guy ride the bull and succeed (in that he didn't entirely fail). So with knees knocking, and my brain berating my body for its pride, I headed for the front of the raft.

Grabbing onto the chicken line, I slipped my legs out in front of me: my center of gravity positioned far over the front of the inflatable pontoon.

I can do this, I chanted silently, as colossal waves began crashing angrily into each other. Suddenly, before I had a second chance to bail out, I was heading down into seemingly the largest trough on the Salmon River.

Abruptly, the raft began riding the crest of a 7-foot wave—what exhilaration; and sense of accomplishment and power. And for a brief moment I felt some of the excitement a real bull rider must experience—without the hooves, the crowd, the danger and the crazy clowns. Riding the white water raft bull was enough for me. I'll leave the sweaty bulls to the short professionals—after all, I still answer to Breezers.

8 reasons pets are better than kids

*R*ecently, my husband and I attended his 10-year high school reunion. I felt a little out of my element, with all the little babies crawling around on the floor dragging a string of drool, while their parents swapped diaper stories.

With each new comment directed my way I was noticing the huge social gap between his classmates and us. Some-one would say: "You should have seen what Jeremiah did when he was only 2 months…." And my reply would be: "That was like when Blitzen (our steer)…" or "Nibbles (our buck) did something similar..." or "And I'd never seen a cat do that until Mr. Murdock …"

Some of our friends and family have expressed their feelings that we have too many animals (both inside and out) and maybe we should have kids instead. For these people, I have considered posting this sign on our gate:

To all non-pet owners who visit and like to complain about our pets:
1. They live here. You don't

2. If you don't want hair on your clothes, stay off the furniture—there's a reason it's called "fur"niture!

And really, in many ways, cats, dogs, sheep and cows are better than kids because they:

1. Don't ask for money.
2. Are easier to potty train.
3. Normally come when called.
4. Never ask to drive the car.
5. Aren't tempted to drink or smoke.
6. Don't have to buy the latest fashions.
7. Don't need money for college.

And last, if they get pregnant—you can sell their children!

Sleep, coffee & dog slobbers

*B*ed is an interesting bundle of paradoxes: we go to it with reluctance at the end of the day—yet we prolong our stay in it the following morning as long as possible. Throughout my life, this has been my story: late to bed and late to rise—I just don't do mornings.

When I was 18, my sister and I lived with my grandparents. Now, my sister is one of those people who get up at 5 a.m. and begin whistling (or would if she could whistle). I on the other hand, figured since school didn't start until 8:05 a.m. and it took 5 minutes to shower and 3 minutes to drive to school, getting up at 7:55 gave me 2 minutes to spare.

My grandpa would come in from changing sprinklers and holler up the stairs "...much longer and Sleeping Beauty becomes Lay-a-Bed Ugly!" I think that was supposed to persuade me to get out of bed, but it has as much effect as my parents' futile attempts. My mom would turn on the lights and threaten us with ice cubes. My dad would flop our mattresses up and down, and when that would fail, he'd take the covers.

All of which probably would have worked had I not grown up a farm kid, learning early on how to curl up in that small space behind the tractor seat and take a nap—sleeping through bumps and squealing belts all the while using ether cans for pillows. That talent has served me well over the years: I can sleep on the floor of the swather, on the toolbox of a pickup, on top of watermelon bins and even on cramped airplanes.

Our first harvest season of marriage, my husband would gently touch my shoulder and whisper that the dew was just right. Over time, those caresses became shoves and the whispers shouts. He even tried calling my cellphone and bringing me hot cocoa. With results as ineffective as were my parents' and grandparents'.

All was going well for my sleep...until one morning while I was enjoying a calorie-free cup of dream-produced espresso, a cold wet nose wriggled its way under my arms and a slobbery tongue began licking my forehead. My dream coffee spilled onto my dream pajamas as I jumped out of bed. An impish husband and happy dog greeted me.

Now just the sound of doggy patters on the floor, can raise me out of a deep sleep. And I've discovered that dog slobber is every bit as stimulating as black coffee—and just as hard to sleep after!

Fleecing the dog...

*T*he cow says moo and the dog says baa? A few years ago, the late Paul Harvey told his audience that "for what it's worth" many people had been fleeced into buying furry, white poodles, that turned out to be furniture-eating sheep. Another story also circulated about a Japanese actress who also bought a fuzzy poodle. She took it to the vet when she couldn't get it to eat dog food or bark...and surprise, her little poodle was a hoofed herbivore.

Sometimes these stories seem so far-fetched...like the stories of kids thinking chocolate milk comes from brown cows. But there I was, talking to a close friend about how the wheel line mover had broke. After listening politely he asked "What is a wheel line?"

I paused a second before answering "a hand line on wheels."

Which raised the next question, "And a hand line would be...?" I really had to scratch my head on that one. How could a person live in the Palouse area for 4 years and not have any idea what irrigation pipe was?

Recently, my sister, a New Jersey resident, was helping a friend move. And as so often happens when relocating, non-moving friends become the proud owners of "new-to-them junk" that the movers don't feel like packing.

"I don't know where this came from, or even what the design means, but you're welcome to it if you want," he said, tossing her a beach towel with the Snap On logo printed across it.

"Oh, it's a Snap On tool logo," my sister said.

"Yeah, whatever that is," he said shrugging his shoulders.

Oh boy. And it's not just an isolated incident. During some casual conversation, another friend asked my sister how many watermelons my family grows. She responded in acres (as any farmer would). Her friend said, no, she wanted to know how many "watermelons" my family grew. As in individual melons!

Another friend said they didn't know what an acre was, how many football fields would they farm? I suppose that would depend on how many players they wanted to grow!

This problem extends beyond farm life and very quickly into common sense. Another friend of my sister's also found herself moving recently. She hired a moving company to transport her furniture.

Upon arriving at her new apartment the professional movers couldn't fit her queen bed up the stairs and into the bedroom. "But it's not a problem," she told my sister while she flipped through the yellow pages, "the movers said I should just call someone to cut the bed in half, move it upstairs and bracket it together."

I think she'll find a bed-bracketing contractor right next to the ad for baa baa black dogs and strawberry milk cows.

It's in the bag...er...pouch

I've heard mothers say how lucky female octopus are. Well I never gave it much thought until I found myself at the sink preparing tomatoes to freeze. Balancing Baby in my left arm (because he wants to see what's happening) while washing and dicing the fruit with my right, I began to understand how nice it would be to have 6 extra arms.

It took longer than usual, but eventually the tomatoes and peppers were stacked in colorful bags in my freezer. While I stood in the open freezer door admiring my hard work, Baby suddenly needed an immediate diaper change.

We measure how bad diapers are on a scale of 1 to 10 wipes This was an 8-wiper. And to make it even more challenging, the little munchkin wanted to look at the floor, the ceiling, the dog—anything to twist and squirm. Hasn't someone said "more hands make less wipes?" Well maybe not, but they should have.

The fresh diaper was barely installed, when my Little One scooted down and was off. Since he still hasn't mastered his balance, I guess it would be more accurate to say "we were off." Baby first, then my finger, and me bringing up the rear. Around and around we went—using his 3 speeds indiscriminately: fast, slow and stop to taste. After a few hours of walking bent over, I was ecstatic to see Daddy pull in the driveway.

As I watched Baby pull his father around (and around) the house, I began to think about evolution; if that theory really was true, I don't think moms would be growing octopus arms, I think they would develop pouches—here's why.

Kangaroos have a 33-day gestation period (nice, since I puked for 6 months), then they crawl into their mother's pouch and attach themselves to a teat where they eat and grow about 6 months. (Again, nice. They eat unassisted, and there's no need to find a private spot for feeding). After that they start to spend time out of the pouch, coming back to mama to eat or sleep. The kangaroo also has short arms ensuring she never has to walk her little one around, which means no backaches for her.

The octopus may have 8 arms, but she lays over 200,000 eggs (the kangaroo rarely has more than 1) which she cares for alone; guarding against predators and blowing water currents over them to ensure they get enough oxygen. She also doesn't eat for nearly a month while she takes care of the eggs—and around the time the eggs hatch—she dies.

Forget the octopus—with 200,000 eggs, she probably wishes she had 80 arms. Add to that the idea of starving to death...ahhhh. Let those other moms wish themselves into starving octopus, I'm working on a pouch and teaching Baby to answer to Joey.

Sunlamps and chickens

$\mathcal{W}$atch what you say. It will be used later. George had died. His lawyer is standing before the family and reads out his Last Will and Testament:

"To my dear wife, I leave the house, 50 acres, and 1 million dollars. To my son I leave my Lexus and the Jaguar. To my daughter, I leave my yacht and $250,000. To my brother-in-law, who always insisted that health is better than wealth, I leave my sunlamp."

Mind your mouth. I haven't ended up with a sunlamp… yet…but it is funny (kind of) how the things you say boomerang back to you. A few months ago, I was chatting with a friend over a cup of coffee, when she said how nice it would be to have a few chickens, but her husband would never go for it. I nodded, and murmured something that was agreeable and (I thought) non-committal. A few days later the chicken topic came up again….this time the point was made that I have an empty chicken coop. Again, I nodded and mumbled something that I hoped couldn't pass for words.

It soon became clear that my ambiguous mumbling was getting me into the chick business.

I supposed it wouldn't be too bad, after all they eat bugs and kitchen scraps, and I love a good egg. Soon, we were talking numbers. We decided that 5 or 6 chickens would give us plenty of eggs. I was thinking 3 or 4, but, in for a penny, in for a pound.

We went into town separately to get the chicks (and here's where my vague mumbling interfered again.) Remember I was thinking 5 or 6? Well I thought that was total....my friend thought that was apiece. And she'd picked up a few extras besides! And if that wasn't enough chickens, my husband rented out the coop to a lady who brought 50 more bundles of fluff!

The moral? Watch what you say (or don't say)...it'll always come back—sometimes in a sunlamp, sometimes in a clucking flock of chickens!!

Lessons by the threes

$\mathcal{B}$ad things are said to happen in threes. I wonder why that is? If you're going to coin a phrase, why not make it more palatable, like: "bad things happen every three years," or "three bad things will happen in your lifetime."

It was a Friday night, and I was trying to get the last minute things done before sundown and the beginning of my Sabbath. There were 20 minutes left of daylight, and 21 things on my grocery list—I'd be pushing sundown—but maybe if I hurried...?

I scooped up my little munchkin and was racing off to the car—when I suddenly heard bleating from behind the garage. I dropped my purse into the seat of my car and hurried around the building.

There was my little flock of sheep—happily munching away on grass far away from their pen on the other side of the garage. After checking the fence—I discovered the gate was wide open—later observation found them to be able to release the horseshoe latch with their noses.

Most of my sheep were bummer lambs—which means they don't herd real well, and they often have selective hearing if you call them to follow—this was one of those times. We went around the house, into the garage, around my car, back around the house… I had sweat running down my face, and they had mischief written on theirs.

I had just stopped to catch a breath, when Doug, a friend of my husband drove in with his two daughters. Never had I been more happy to see him or his girls. Soon the chase was on again….

Suddenly, I heard a "Moo, moo, moo." I came around the corner of the house, to see Doug waving his arms and hollering, trying to get the steer back into his pen. How had that rotten critter got out? I wondered. I panicked for a moment, looking for my little baby. It's one thing for sheep to be running around with him on the loose—but a 1,000-pound steer was another thing entirely.

My Little One was still standing near my car—and laughing. I guess I should have been happy that someone was finding amusement in this poor comedy of errors. I had barely snatched him up when a scream pierced the air.

"The dog has a chicken!!" There was Illy, with my favorite hen in her mouth. It was my turn to wave my arms and holler.

I had to pry her mouth open to release the chicken—who surprisingly got up and waddled away unscathed—which is more than I can say for my dog who had to spend the remainder of the night in the garage (her worst punishment is being penned up).

Soon Old McDonald's farm was put away for the night and I leaned up against my car door—now well past sundown, and sighed deeply. Three events had taught 3 lessons: 1st: Bad things really do happen in three's. 2nd: Don't even try to push Friday night sundown…those 21 items aren't worth it. 3rd: I don't know why they need "do not" signs—only the most skilled drivers can make a ewe-turn anyway.

Me and the goat

It was time to milk the goat. I put on a ratty sweatshirt and old pair of jeans and stepped into the brisk winter air. An old white bowl was squeezed under my elbow as I let myself through the gate. The poor thing came waddling up to me, hardly able to walk around her large udder. We had just sold her babies, and I was surprised to see that she was still making copious amounts of milk. So here I was to relieve some of her misery.

I singled her out, and we squeezed out of the gate together, leaving a bunch of unhappy unchosens behind. Putting corn in a little bucket, my husband came over to help hold her. I slipped the bowl underneath her and began my lovely visions of stream after stream filling the bowl with warm frothy milk.

She would be relieved and thankful to me; I would scratch her back, and we would both look at each other while soft music filled the air, and we shared a special bonding moment. From then I would divide the milk between the cats, and perhaps even take some home to see if I may even like the taste, and all of this would happen to a beautiful sunrise, bathing everything in a soft, red light.

As soon as my chilly hands touched her bag, she jerked

away from my husband's loose grasp, bleated an alarm and stepped into the bowl. We tried it again. Same thing, different order. Again. Again. A never-before-been-milked goat, coupled with a never before-goat milker, fills a book with funny stories, but a bowl with nothing but straw and dirt.

We finally got her up against a fence, and finally got her milk to let down. And down it came. Everywhere except in the bowl. Streams went shooting into my stomach, onto my boots, and into the cat's face—who didn't seem to mind. As soon as milk finally splattered into the plastic bowl, she would either step into it, or kick it over, what did stay in the bowl, was getting soaked up by all the straw she had kicked in.

I finally gave up on the bowl...and began milking her out on the ground. She kept flipping her head over her back and giving me the angry eye. The dog and cats sat scowling with each stream of milk that splattered wastefully into the ground. The sunrise wasn't a beautiful red...or if it was I couldn't see it over the heavy fog that had settled in. The whole vision was going up in smoke, like the steam from the milk-soaked soil.

Her bag finally soft, I put her back in the pasture and closed the gate. I put the empty plastic bowl back under my arm and headed for the house, nothing to show for my efforts but wet sticky clothes. Next time sugar plums start dancing in my head, I think I'll go back to bed and wait for those 8 maids a milking to stop by my house and show me how it's done.

The farmer's raffle

*O*nce upon a time, a farmer sold a horse to a passing gentleman. After agreeing on a price, the gentleman said he would pick it up in the morning.

Unfortunately, when the gentleman arrived the next morning, he discovered it had died during the night. The farmer was distraught, and offered the gentleman back his money.

But he shook his head, "No. I told you I'd buy the horse, and a gentleman always keeps his word." So saying, he loaded up the dead horse and drove away. A couple of weeks later, the farmer saw the gentleman in town, "Whatever happened with that horse?" he asked.

"I sold it and made a fortune," the gentleman replied.

Astonishment covered the farmer's face, "You sold it? How?"

"A raffle."

"That must've made a few people angry..." the farmer stammered.

"No, only one—but I refunded his money."

It seems everyone nowadays has some sort of a scheme to live the American Dream with as little effort as possible.

All one has to do is turn on the television and myriad programs come on promising to make you a millionaire with three 30-minute CD's— and 36 easy installments of $54.95 a month. Or maybe the commercial is about a diet pill (or patch, or cream, or gel, or injection, or tea, or...) that will help you shed those unwanted pounds without any dieting or exercise.

There is no end to the types of products that will heal disease, prevent disease, grow hair, prevent hair, lose weight, gain muscles, and make you money—with little or no effort from you.

One of the latest schemes I've encountered is the miracle of coconut oil. While there may be some very valuable benefits to using coconut oil, I just can't bring myself to believe all the characteristics the promoters push.

They claim it promotes weight loss, protects against heart disease, cancer, diabetes, arthritis, and many other degenerative diseases. It also prevents premature aging of the skin, beautifies the hair, and strengthens the immune system, as well as aiding in overcoming the flu. Although there is no standard dosage for eating coconut oil to combat the flu, they recommend 4-8 tablespoons a day "until you feel better." It is such a miracle elixir; one can use it as a topical cream, in cooking, or just a couple spoonfuls at a time if you're feeling low.

I'm not disagreeing with all of their claims...but there sure are a lot of them. And my dad always told me "If it's too good to be true...you can bet your last melon it is."

And since so many of them require so many "easy monthly payments" you'll be paying through the nose for their schemes, maybe buying a dead horse isn't so bad. Both men profited, and most of the raffle losers never knew they spent money on a dead horse.

Speaking of which—there's an old dead horse up on the hill...I won it.

Hello, goodbye Mr. Billy

"**M**omma, come, come," my Little One motioned as soon as I stepped out of my Jeep. "Hurry, Momma, come." He turned, and began his determined stride across the lawn. We reached the fence, and he pointed to the goats in the pasture. "Mama goat kiss Daddy goat. Daddy goat happy!"

My laughter contrasted his most serious expression. The day before my grandpa had brought me a billy goat to breed my two nannies. And standing there watching them, I supposed the 'daddy goat' was quite 'happy.' And if that is happy, I hope that my Little One is miserable until he's graduated college!

The 'daddy goat' novelty lasted all week for my 3-year-old. Every time we were outside, he wanted to see if they were still 'happy.' He's been around sheep his whole life, but a major difference between my sheep and the goats... the sheep are much more discreet, while the goats seem to enjoy making a spectacle of themselves...which my Little One found fascinating.

Much more fascinating than I did. The goats were loud, and the billy...wow...that's some cologne! But, just like the neighbor's donkey and our six roosters, we quickly learned to ignore them...that is until we came home one day and Mr. Billy was nibbling contentedly outside the pasture. He obligingly went back in, and all was well—for another hour.

While washing dishes, I glanced out the window, and Mr. Billy was eating the trees that line my driveway. I was a little annoyed, but he went back in so easily, all was forgiven before I'd reached the chicken coop to gather the eggs. I'd barely set the cartons down on the counter, when I glanced out the window…and saw Mr. Billy eating my rose bushes in the yard. I stomped back outside, and grumpily chased him back into the pasture.

Upon reaching the house, I heard my little boy crying. He'd woke up from his nap to an empty house and he was scared. He opened the door and I scooped him up.

"Momma, goat out," he sniffled. I turned, and sure enough, Mr. Billy was already ambling peacefully into the alfalfa field. With a groan, I returned to a losing game.

I marched out there, a toddler on one hip, determination oozing through every pore, and Mr. Billy looked up and ran for the opened gate.

I smiled smugly to myself…never mess with a tired mother…and that was when my nose decided to gush blood, and the goat decided to jump over the gate…he didn't even have the decency to wait until I turned my back.

Mr. Billy didn't stay his full 30 days here. And as my grandpa pulled out of the driveway with him, I snuggled up to my husband, "kissing Daddy goat goodbye…makes this Momma happy!!"

What does AI mean to you?

"*H*e's hurting her! Do something," her kids cried. My friend's face blanched. She looked mortified, and I could tell she was wishing those chickens anywhere but in my lawn. "Um, well, er, ah…," she stammered. Her kids looked up expectantly, but nothing more was coming out of her mouth. I smothered a giggle when my son tried to explain that they were just…playing.

It was a nice sunny afternoon—one in which the sheep seemed to be feeling their oats—and the young buck seemed especially amorous. For my friend it was a day of questions and awkward stammers. They had come over to see the baby lambs frolic in the pasture, and to feed Bummer, the preemie that lived in a box in my kitchen. They had not come to learn about the birds chasing the bees.

I had never really noticed when the roosters paid the hens attention, much less felt the need to blush. And when the ewes were mounted, it wasn't something to turn away from in embarrassment, instead it usually made the evening dinner conversation: "I saw the buck mounting Dirty Harry this morning…and he was starting to follow Junior tonight…I think he only has a few more girls left to go."

If letting her kids see animals in their natural state was

embarrassing I wondered what she would think if she saw farm kids involved in A.I.? Then again, would she even know what A.I was? Just for fun, I sent out a mass text asking to name the first thing one thought when I said A.I. It was so interesting. Every person with an ag background responded with: cattle impregnation, semen, work, cows, and of course Artificial Insemination.

The majority of non-aggies responded with Artificial Intelligence, although some answered with: American Idol, steak sauce, guns, and one response read "hot tub" (I was afraid to ask what that meant!)

After I quit laughing from some of the responses I started to process the information. Kids raised on farms often begin their sex ed before they can walk or talk. They learn about it around their parents in a straightforward and non-plussed way. There is no blushing or embarrassment. It's just reproduction. It is also holistic in a way that sex ed from a book can never be. They see more than just fuzzy baby lambs romping on their mother's backs, baby chicks following their mother to scratch for bugs, and baby calves licking their fingers through the gate.

Farm kids have seen babies pulled when things don't progress smoothly, mouth-to-mouth to keep babies from dying, and most have experienced feeding those bummers around the clock.

There's something about getting out of a warm bed, mixing milk and traipsing out to the barn every few hours to feed babies that don't want to eat, that I think is one of the most important parts of sex ed—it seems to eliminate baby fever—and makes abstinence look like the only choice.

So when my son becomes a teenager, I think I'm going to invest in several hundred bummers every year for him to take care of!

Sheep, gauges, & suggestions

I rushed out the door for work…and saw two of my little woolly friends out for a morning stroll in my lawn. Late as usual, I thought about chasing them in, but figured "easy come, easy go." I let them be and gave a quick glance to my gauges as I slid behind the wheel of my Jeep.

The fuel gauge was close to E, but nothing to worry about—it wasn't as if I was going a long way…only 35 miles or so… And the light wasn't on—yet—it didn't come on until I had just left the city limits. But I wasn't concerned, I can still go another 30+ miles after it lights up. I thought about getting fuel when I got to town, but I was already late—so I hurried to the office instead.

Just as I was leaving work I got a phone call from a friend I hadn't talked to in years. By the time I got off the phone, I had filled up on memories and never thought about filling up the tank. I was part way home before that pesky orange light in the corner of the dash caught my eye.

My fuel needle had departed E some time ago, and I was nowhere near a gas station. I'd like to say the empty fuel tank anxiety was a new feeling to me—but it's not. I drive most of my miles on the bottom half of the tank, and quite often it's the last quarter. I've always viewed E as more of a suggestion and the idiot light as peer pressure. But this time I should have listened. I pulled over at the bottom of a wide hill and that's when I heard my cellphone's battery beep— I've kind of always viewed that as a suggestion too.

Luckily, I had enough to make one phone call before it scrolled "goodbye" across its screen. Hours later, when I pulled into the driveway, I had to stop for those same lambs that were enjoying their food from the other side of the fence. I beeped the horn a couple of times and watched them scurry for the gate.

Those two lambs get out every day and help themselves to the roses, the bushes, the trees, the alfalfa, the silage, my flower pots—whatever seems to strike their fancy. And so far, no fence repairs have been able to keep them in. Then it dawned on me—they saw the fence as just a suggestion— and none of us seem to be very good at taking those suggestions seriously.

The blood, the mud, the gore

The sun reflected brightly off the hood of my mom's car as she pulled into my driveway. She was earlier than I was expecting and I wasn't quite dressed for our mother-daughter afternoon. I shoved my feet into my rubber boots and zipped up the legs of my coveralls. I grabbed a pair of gloves on my way out the door to meet her. We fore-went any "normal" mother/daughter hugs as she had come straight from working cows and her clothes smelled almost as organic as mine did.

I had a ewe that was having some serious birthing prob-lems and I had done the best thing I knew how: I'd called my mom.

We headed into the barn where we laughed, then nearly cried; told funny stories, shared gossip, and did all those things that mothers and daughters usually do. Only instead of Chanel No. 5, our aroma was more like Corral No. 5. And instead of a table with cups of tea or coffee on it, we had a couple of buckets of warm water, several bottles of dish soap, and a partially birthed dead lamb in lieu of a conversation piece.

More unexpected problems had us scrolling down our contact lists attempting to enlist help. Soon another lady from the neighborhood came bearing more lubricant and calf pullers. But luck was not on our side, and after a while, the neighbor went home. And my mom and I leaned back against the wood boards of the pen and tried to regroup.

There we were kneeling in a barn jug, both of us tired, frustrated and covered in birthing fluids. I watched bloody soap drip down my mom's forearms and I could see the her hand swelling from the intense pulling.

I suddenly realized that even though it was unortho-dox...this was our bonding time. This kind of event had always been our thing. From early on in my childhood, I have memories of traipsing out to the barn in the middle of the night behind my mom, to pull a lamb, check on a ewe, suture up a sheep after dogs got in, and once even taking lambs caesarian. Some mothers and daughters might go to the movies or go shopping, or get a mani-pedi. But that wasn't us, we had always bonded over life and death situa-tions—most often ones that smelled bad.

In that moment I had A Boy Named Sue feeling. Sue has finally met his dad and after a drag-out fight, and he says: *"I got all choked up and I threw down my gun. I called him my pa, and he called me his son. I came away with a dif-ferent point of view. I think about him every now and then. Every time I try and every time I win. And if I ever have a son, I think I'm gonna name him...Bill or George!! Any-thing but Sue!"*

As serious as the situation was, I couldn't help but smile...if I ever have a daughter, I'm gonna bond over cof-fee or shopping...anything but blood!

Kids

I think that if you were raised on a farm,
you were born with dirt in your shoes.
And once you get dirt in your shoes...
you can't ever get it out.

Not the toys of yesterday...

*K*ids today just don't play like they used to. I remember going to visit my cousins over Christmas. They had the most cool dirt hole out behind their house. Over the years the dirt hole grew–the living area (or the waiting room, or the economy cabin, or the spy headquarters) was probably 5 feet in diameter, and from there we had dug multiple tunnels. Some of these caved it...but enough stayed put so that we had many other avenues of play.

Some days we were prisoners of war trying to tunnel out, other days we were miners looking to strike it rich–sometimes I think we really believed we would find the mother lode.

Usually it got too cold to be out late into the evening, but I do remember a few occasions digging by flashlight... often fussing when my aunt would call us into the house.

Today, I'm not sure how many kids would get excited about playing in a dirt hole–no matter how many tunnels it had–unless it was on PlayStation and you were scored for how many tunnels you'd dug and how long each one lasted.

Recently, I was getting a lesson on buying a gaming system from a 10-year-old. He was telling me the pros and cons of each one...ending his unsolicited lecture with:

"But don't buy the Xbox 360–the resolution is real poor."

I had to laugh…I'm pretty sure when I was 10 the only thing I knew about resolution was associated with New Year's.

But kids today are different. That point was really driven home the other night while Christmas shopping at Toys R Us. We stopped for a bit to let our Little One drool over the big 12-volt plastic cars. He went immediately to the tractor, and while he raised and lowered the loader, we strolled through the beefy Jeeps, and pink Barbie cars.

That's when I realized that most of the cars had working FM radios, and many had real CD and MP3 players!! In the kiddie cars!!! My first real car only had an a.m. radio–and it didn't even work. But I was so excited just to drive–I barely noticed.

I haven't decided if it's because kids today are just more sophisticated that we were—or their parents just have more credit cards. Either way, I'm sure they wouldn't be thrilled with a new shovel even if it did come with blueprints for a bigger hole come Christmas.

The wisdom of kids

*H*ave you ever considered the vast wisdom in the innocence of a child's thoughts? My mom once overheard two of her girls talking over a Bible book of creation—in which Adam and Eve are cleverly painted behind rose bushes.

"Why don't Adam and Eve have any clothes on?" the youngest girl asked.

The other answered: "because, sewing machines weren't invented yet." Of course!!

I teach the 6-10 year-olds at my church. Recently, we were studying Daniel and the lions' den. At the end of class, I offered extra credit for anyone who wrote a fable about a lion. The following week I was blown away by some of the morals they gave. The following story and moral were written by a girl named Makenzi.

THE STORY: *Once upon a time there was a lion named Leo. Everyone thought he was ferocious but he wasn't. One day Leo's trainer opened his gate. He was so sick of being at the zoo—he wanted to go. So he leaped right over the trainer.*

"Leo escaped!" cried everyone. Leo was going down the street and everyone was scared.

But little, teeny, tiny Suzi who was three-and-a-half, wasn't afraid. She thought he was a kitty. She petted and petted him. She got some rope and tied it around his neck.

Leo and little Suzi went in the store where her mom was. She asked her ,om if she could keep him. They did and lived happily ever after.

THE MORAL: *This lesson is about Suzi's mom not judging people or animals on the outside. And, don't leave your children outside alone.*

Simple—yet profound. It makes me wonder why I'm teaching the class—with wisdom like that, maybe my job description should be crowd-control...it might be more accurate anyway!

Idioms redefined

*H*eaven's to Betsy! An American phrase has been in circulation since the latter part of the 19th century, although its use faded throughout the 20th century and it is now something of an anachronism.

I love idioms, they take us back to our roots in a way that no history book can. Like shoofly pie. Easy to imagine those hot southern afternoons, with gooey molasses pies sitting on the counters attracting flies.....

This week I found new meanings to many of those idioms as I watched my son and nephew (both 2), play outside in the dirt hole.

•*Keep your chin up.* The boys would tilt their faces to the sun, then throw handfuls of dirt up in the air and watch as the particles landed in their eyes.

•*On the rocks.* Other family members had stopped to visit, and most of us had cups of soda pop in our hands. My back was turned to the little boys, when suddenly, plop, my nephew dunked a handful of gravel into my glass. Squirt on the rocks.

•On the fence. Still chatting with our visitors, I was startled to see my brother-in-law running toward the sheep pasture…and the little boys standing at the top of the gate. Luckily, he got there before my nephew did the "look dad, no hands" trick.

•Cut a rug. What better thing for little boys to play with than tractors, trucks, and other farm machinery. So my son, was playing with his combine in the grass. It wasn't very long before he moved to the sidewalk, specifically the rug at the foot of the porch. I asked if the rug was more fun to play on, he nodded, and said, "cut better."

• A chip on your shoulder. Snack time consisted of juice and crackers in the dirt hole. Ryan, my nephew, seemed ravenous, and crackers were flying everywhere. Upon pointing out a cracker stuck under his collar, he paused a moment… then ate it. Hmmmm….there's got to be a moral in that somewhere.

•Kitty corner. 2 little boys herding a litter of kittens into the corner of their dirt hole.

•Bite off more than you can chew. How much cookie can a boy cram into his mouth at once? I'm not sure I know, but the dog seemed pretty willing for them to keep repeating their experiment.

•A leopard can't change his spots. Well, obviously he'd never met a 2-year-old with a paint brush and momma's supply of paint.

After the boys had been scrubbed and tucked into bed, I put on my slippers, grabbed a book and headed for the rocking chair incurring the last definition…this aunt rocks!!

Alfalfa sprouts...

*K*ids don't get enough credit for having their own priorities. Parents think if they push here and pull there, they can shape their kid into "what's best for him/her." Unfortunately though, those kids seem to have a mind of their own.

Take my munchkin for example. We began reading to him soon after he was born. I had flash cards for him as well. I was sure he would say Mommy before long. Instead, he began to say "tra-tor" (tractor) and not another word, (not even a jabber that I could interpret as mama). He created his own sign language for anything else he needed.

Shortly after he turned 2, we were in the car, waiting for my husband to run some errands, and soon exhausted our supply of books. So I began my ongoing quest of trying to get him to say mommy, mama, mom or any other variation of mother. He just shook his head.

"Say Mommy," I cooed, tickling his tummy. He continued to shake his head no.

After a couple of minutes of this, he looked over at me, squinted his eyes, and giggled, "Daddee." He then covered his mouth and belly laughed.

For months, no matter how hard I've tried to get him

to say Mommy (or cat, dog, cow or horse), he only said 2 words: Daddy and Tractor…priorities.

Last night while serving supper, we set an alfalfa sprout sandwich on my son's plate. My Little One, looked at the bagel, lifted off the top half, and began a thorough study of the sprouts. Finally, he tilted his head, looked up at me and said, "Momma, hay! Goats, hay. Cows, hay. Me, hay."

Everything he does revolves around farming. He prefers tractors to cars. He prefers tools over toys, and would wear his work boots to bed if I'd let him. When playing trucks, he'll often lift them up on the floor jack so he can "fix them."

Many people think that kids are just lumps of raw clay waiting for you to shape and mold them into your choosing. I'm not so sure. He chooses tractor documentaries over cartoons, boots instead of my preferred sandals, and he even passes up the pool to ride in the combine. If he is a lump of clay…I'm sure he's green, and tractor-shaped.

World of farming

$\mathcal{E}$verything in my world revolves around farming. Vacations are taken after the last of the winter wheat is planted and before spring ground work begins. Shop work is done on rainy days so as not to waste valuable sunshine.

Our wedding date was planned for those reasons, as was the birth of our little boy. When choosing toys, the most logical ones are tractors, plows and shovels; our household reading material is ag newspapers, farm classifieds, and of course the *Fastline.*

All of these things are just commonplace and I've never really thought twice about them...until I realized what an impact they were making on my son, Keagan. The first was while I was paying bills and he saw the invoice from Napa. He pointed to their logo and said "Ooh, Momma, candy store." I was confused for a moment or two, before my husband reminded me about the candy dish they have sitting on their counter. Later, he was talking about going to the "toy store"—which turned out to be the local John Deere store. Forget Sees Candy, or Toys-'R-Us they don't have this little boy's interest.

Recently, we were sitting on the kitchen floor playing with blocks. He was loading the blocks onto a semi-trailer through the aid of a hay squeeze…I used to (erroneously) use it as a large hair clip…but *"Keagan Blue Book"* (not to be mistaken for *Kelly Blue Book*) now lists it as a 'hay squeeze.'

Keagan pushed an empty trailer towards me and handed me the 'squeeze' to load it with. I picked up a block with the hair clip and said "Red rectangle."

Keagan shook his head and took it away from me. He set it on the truck and said "Big Bale!" He then pointed out each of the rectangles in the pile and "Big Bale." I tried a few more times to teach him rectangles and squares, but quickly gave up. It didn't matter what color, to him they were only 'big bales' or 'little bales.' I picked up a cylinder, thinking I could teach him shapes if we got away from 'bales.' He reached out and took it away from me saying "Silly Momma, round bales!"

Last weekend we went up snowmobiling and I'd left our helmets on the counter. So I was only mildly surprised when I walked in on a little helmet bobble head in the living room. He was making funny noises in the oversize helmet, so I stopped to watch him a moment. That's when I noticed the play welder in his gloved hands. He must have sensed my presence, for he stood up, lifted the shield on the helmet and offered to show me the "fixed plow."

I guess his world revolves around farming too, after all his very first gift in this world was a pair of rubber irrigation boots from my parents—and a pair of custom-made baby hay hooks from the neighbor. I wouldn't be surprised if someday he, too, plans his vacations, wedding, and babies around a farming schedule.

No question about it...

*I*t was inevitable, but for some reason I thought we would beat it. I was wrong. It started as any other summer day in the northwest: hot, dusty, and filled with farm work. It wasn't how it started, but rather how it ended, that will forever make August 2, 2012, a date to be remembered.

I swiped at a trickle of sweat making mud down my forehead as I unbuckled my 3-year-old and pulled him out of my Jeep. We were both covered in dirt and wheat chaff and quite possibly too dirty to go into the store.

But I'd promised him his favorite snack if he didn't complain about his 10 hours in the combine today. So now we were on a mission for a bag of apples.

I slid his feet through the holes of the kid seat in the cart and started pushing toward the produce section and inevitability. I quickly scanned the prices on the apples and settled for the sale apples. My little boy looked up at me and pointed to the fujis. I shook my head no, "They're more expensive Sweetie," I told him, and started bagging the granny smiths.

"Why Momma?" he asked.

"Because these one's are on sale."

"Why?"

"Because the store had too many of them and wanted to

get rid of them faster," I made up.

"Why?"

"Because if they have too many apples they might spoil."

"Why?"

"Because when fruit gets old it rots; like when watermelons sit outside too long and they get really mushy."

"Why?"

"Because of the enzymes...." I suddenly realized I had just entered a new stage. A terrifying, mouth-drying-because-you're-talking-too-much stage. I spent the next hour explaining everything from ignition switches to pick-up reels.

My grandmother always told me if I couldn't amaze 'em with brilliance, baffle 'em with bull.... I always thought she was being funny, but now I see she was just preparing me for all the "whys and wherefores" of life with inquisitive children.

After a few weeks of being assaulted with the "W" word, I'm thankful both for my grandmother's wisdom and the rubber boots my husband bought me. Why, you question?

Well I'm really glad you asked, because I'm getting quite proficient at answering questions to which I am clueless... maybe I should quit farming and go into politics!

Old McDonald retired

"*She'll be driving a John Deere tractor when she comes. She'll be driving a John Deere tractor, she'll be driving a John Deere tractor, she'll be driving a John Deere tractor when she comes,*" my little boy and I sang. We were cultivating, and like the many hours in the tractor I had spent growing up with my mom, we were passing the time singing folk songs.

Only my Little One didn't like the traditional verses, so we sang: "She will hook the plow to the tractor when she comes."

"She will swath the hay in rows, for it to dry."

"She will rake and bale the hay to make feed."

"She will load the truck with the squeeze, when she comes."

I tried some of my old favorites: wearing red pajamas and eating chicken and dumplings—it was a definite no. After an hour or more, "She" had driven every piece of machinery we had owned. Then my little boy looked up at me with big questioning eyes and asked, "Who is She?"

I had no idea what to tell him....obviously she was superwoman knowing how to drive all that machinery. And then he asked me where "She" lived.

"I don't know. Where do you think she lives?"

He looked thoughtful for just a moment before he answered "Disneyland!"

I just enjoy seeing the world through his eyes; it's always a new—and often a learning—adventure. Soon we were singing his rendition of Old McDonald. On his farm he had a "tractor, plow, squeeze, black truck, blue truck, cultivator and swather."

Have you ever tried to make noises for all of the implements. I can do a little *vroom vroom* or a chug-a-chugga for a tractor or truck—but what noise does a plow or cultivator make? After really struggling with a sound for harrow, I sang the next verse about a mouse. I hadn't even got to the "Eek Eek here and an Eek Eek there" yet, before my Little One was tugging at my arm.

"No Momma, McDonald no have mice on his farm, only tractors!" That's when realization dawned on me—Old McDonald was Old and probably retired by now; and McDonald Junior prefers to deal in equipment rather than cows.

The three-year-old mind often gives us a wild ride. Sometimes amazing us at its insight, other times surprising us with humor, but always making us wonder "where did that came from?"

Earlier this fall, our Little One asked one of our friends to tell him a story about when he was a little kid. After indulging him in quite a long tale, our Little One asked for "another story."

That's when our friend tilted his head and asked, "Why don't you tell me a story about when you were a little kid?" Our Little One sat back in his chair, a look of intense thought across his face.

Then he replied: "One day, long, long time, I in Momma's tummy—then I came out!" And now you know, in the famous words of Paul Harvey, the rest of the story…

Magicians, & rabbit traps

$\mathcal{P}$laying outside was one of the most enjoyable parts of growing up in a farming family: stomping in mud puddles, building dirt roads, using sticks to "cultivate" fields, eating locust blossoms, staining your feet green by running barefoot in fresh-cut grass and drinking out of the hose when you got thirsty.

And as long as you weren't in your "church clothes," you didn't have to worry about your mom scolding you for coming in with green knees, bloody elbows, and muddy brown socks.

We didn't always have fancy toys to play with, but we never minded—a simple stick could be an oar in an Indian canoe, or a musketeer sword, or Christopher Columbus' telescope. And one could do amazing things with a stick, some string and a sheet snuck outside past your mom.

Recently my 3-year-old was outside playing cowboys and magicians. Running around the yard throwing baler twine ropes, and then pulling pretend rabbits out of his cowboy hat. He was hollering a mixture of "yee-haw!" and "presto!"

After a bit he came in and asked for some carrots. He didn't want to eat them in the house, so he went trotting outside with a paper plate full of baby carrots. A bit later, he burst into the house, "Momma, Momma, come!!" he shouted, grabbing my hand and pulling me outside. Right in the middle of the yard was an interesting looking contraption. A black milk crate balanced precariously on a wooden stake that had green baler twine wrapped around it and a long tail leading away from it.

He was dancing around and pointing excitedly. Looking closer I noticed the plate full of baby carrots underneath the crate. "Look, Momma, look!" he exclaimed, "a rabbit trap!" I covered my mouth with my hand, so he couldn't see me giggle as he excitedly showed me how a rabbit would come to eat the carrots and he would pull the rope, knock down the crate and "trap the rabbit!"

He sat outside holding the end of that baler twine for nearly an hour, before he came trudging in the house. "Rabbits not hungry yet," he stated. For days he tried to catch rabbits, and the closest he came was almost catching an old hen who had wandered into his trap to peck at the carrots.

His determination was so admirable, that my husband and I nearly considered buying a rabbit to put in his trap. But then again, if you give a boy a rabbit, he'll play for a day; but if you let the boy imagine the rabbit, you won't have to deal with the 64,738 rabbits that will soon be wreaking havoc on the neighborhood!

Another dimension of time & space

Sun glinted off the towering 13 floors of the most terrifying elevator I've ever been on. I shivered as I passed the bellhop at the door and waited a moment as my eyes adjusted to the gloom. The interior was even more frightening than the outside: cobwebs covered chandeliers, an old doll lay forgotten on the hotel lobby couch, and a massive concrete bird spread his wings over a dried up fountain. Hauntingly familiar music drifts through the lobby…I have just entered….the Twilight Zone.

I'm ready to turn tail and run, but my little 4-year-old is holding my hand excitedly, ready to ride the Tower of Terror, a Disneyland attraction that is one of my least favorites. It combines two of my greatest fears: heights and falling, and attempts to make them pleasurable. My siblings love this ride, and last year found great enjoyment in packing me on and holding my arms in the air to prevent me from leaving handprints in the iron hand holds. I swore last year, as I wobbled off the ride I would never go anywhere near the Tower again.

And yet here I was, waiting in line for a ride that sends hot fear searing through every bone in my body. I stepped into the ride, buckled up my 4-year-old, then myself and zip-locked my eyes shut. Breathe, breathe, brea—-the ride dropped.

When we finally reached the bottom, I unpeeled the skin from my fingers off the handles in front of me and slowly got my shaking legs up and out of the elevator. Thankfully my son wasn't a huge fan, so he didn't ask to go back…although it could have had something to do with the prints I'd left on his left hand from being between mine and the metal handle….

I just couldn't figure out how a little 4-year-old toe-head could have such persuasive power over me. I've always been stubborn and not easily swayed by popular opinion or peer pressure, one time even earning the name hammer head for my bull-headedness. And he had me willingly going on a ride I know terrifies me?

I watched to make sure that my feet were moving correctly as we shuffled out the door and back into the sunlight. That's when I noticed the pink socks.

For Christmas my son was sure that I would love some hot pink socks, so he convinced his Nana to buy them for me. I hate pink. I hate everything about it. Pink reminds me of Barbies and poodles, damsels in distress and everything else that is weak, wimpy, and dependant. Pink belongs on cupcakes and cookies.

What was I doing wearing those pink Christmas socks, getting off a ride that scares me? But as I looked down into that happy upturned face, I realized I would do so much more for him.…I just hope he doesn't want to drive pink motorcycles or Ford tractors.…it really will be another dimension of time and space and I'll know I've crossed over into The Twilight Zone.…

Snake-killing farmers

"You know you killed two big bull snakes in that field you swathed yesterday?" one of the guys told me while greasing up my swather for the new day.

"Eesh," I answered, "I didn't know I swathed them...but I hate snakes."

"You didn't swath them—they broke their backs from trying to follow you down the row."

It took me a few seconds to process, before he burst with laughter, and I remembered my crooked rows in yesterday's field. My little 4-year-old had felt the time had come to promote him to swather driver—after all he'd been observing since he was 5 weeks old. After asking to drive, he looked up at me with his dirty little John Deere hat, grease-smeared face, and pleading blue eyes, I didn't think twice. I scooped him onto my seat and let him "snake" his way down the alfalfa rows.

And while we probably weren't very fuel-efficient in our "scenic route" rows, it was an enlightening experience. He knew which levers and buttons needed pushed, and I was pleased that he was able to work them all in the correct sequence. The only buttons he needed reminders on, were the radio dials—but I have faith—he'll get there in time.

Forward and back, across the field we went…until he confused me with a question. "What makes money grow up out of ground?"

A few days prior he and a friend had found a coin in the gravel and she gave it to him. I assumed this was what he was referring to, and answered accordingly. He got frustrated, "No, No! Why money grow up from ground?" he asked.

Again I explained how someone had dropped the coin on the ground, it didn't actually grow there. This made my 4-year-old upset. "No! No!" he shouted. "not the coin. Money!"

I was confused; and my confusion fueled his irritation. Finally, slowly, like he was the adult explaining to a very dense child, he pointed to the alfalfa. "See! Money. What makes it grow up from ground?"

I couldn't help but squeeze him in a big hug. He's grown up hearing "it's as good as money in a bale;" and when my husband picks up hay, he doesn't count the bales as they go up the harrowbed chute—he counts the fee he charges to pick it up. So, to my Little ne, hay and money seemed synonymous.

I answered him again, this time I explained what makes alfalfa grow. He was satisfied, and I was proud—my little boy looks like he's well on his way to being a tax-paying, snake-killing, money-growing farmer.

Finger lickin' lies

I lied. I'd told myself I never would lie to him, but I did. The first time I felt bad, but it gets easier. Each time, every day that the lie passes my lips, I squirm just a little less, sometimes I barely notice the untruth unless someone overhears me and gives me a questioning look.

Today however, it seemed even more blatant that usual, and I even tried a different tactic before the bold face lie came across my lips.

I was baling hay, and my little boy was sitting on the greasy floor playing with his toys. I use the term boy, loosely. A more accurate description would be a dirt-shaped likeness of my little boy. The air conditioner wasn't keeping up on the blazing sun through the glass, and sweat was making mud trails down both of our faces.

We'd been in the tractor all day and he had just asked for a snack. I'd pulled out our lunch bag and handed him his favorite "spicy crackers" (spicy Tabasco Cheez-its) and that's when he asked the dreaded question.

"Are my hands clean?"

I don't know where he learned that—certainly not from me. I support the 5-second rule—even 10 seconds if the snack was really tasty; I consider my pocket knife "eater-friendly" after a brisk brush across my jeans; and unless there is poison, pesticides, or manure on my hands, I consider them field-eating clean.

The house rules involve a bit more soap, but until John Deere starts installing sinks beside their buddy seat, most anything in the field goes.

For the last several months, anytime my little guy goes to eat anything: a chip, a cracker, a bowl of green beans—the first thing out of his mouth is "are my hands clean?" Grrr.

At first I would tell him the truth, "no, they are filthy, dirty!" but then he would refuse to eat until they were clean. Quite a tall order when one is in a piece of machinery all day. I tried asking him what he thought...but he wouldn't have it...he had asked me a question, and he expected an answer. I tried nodding as it seemed less like lying than actually verbalizing yes...but no. He wanted a spoken yes or no answer.

So now, I'm looking at my little grub—sweat, and dirt matted his hair back against his cheek. Grease, mud and several unidentified substances covered his little hands that were held out for my inspection. His innocent little eyes looked up at me and asked again, "Are my hands clean, Momma?"

I swallowed hard, before smiling brightly at him, "Yep, sweetie, they are."

Papa's heavenly lessons

*W*e recently returned from a Disneyland vacation with my parents. My husband has a fear of traveling without some kind of return on the trip—which is why we usually eBaycation, instead of joining the rest of the world in a genuine vacation. This time however, he hadn't been the one to find a good buy, it was a local farmer—we were just delivering the good buy. And driving a 25-foot trailer in LA traffic definitely prevents our trip from being a typical family vacation.

But other parts were so typical it was cliché. Like the two boys in the backseat hollering "He touched me!" Toys being thrown back and forth, squealing, and tickling, occasionally followed by silence—which of course meant someone in the front seat was soon to be conked on the head with whatever object was closest to the boys in the backseat. Grandpas and grandsons should never sit together on long trips—because grandpas help grandsons get into mischief they haven't thought of yet!

Although I must admit, that while most of the time they were incorrigible, some interesting conversations came out of it. Driving late one night through Central California, I heard my 4-year-old, ask "Papa, why is the moon following us?"

"Because it likes us," my dad told him.

"Why is the moon following us, Momma?" he asked me.

So I launched into detailed explanation about the moon being so far away, and although trees and such seem to zip by, but the moon is so far away it can give the allusion of following us.

My dad turned and with mock exaggeration asked, "You understand all that?"

He shook his head no.

My dad gave me an "I told you so" look.

"Fine," I sighed exasperatedly, "you explain it."

He smirked. "I did. The moon likes us!"

And suddenly I remembered a conversation I'd had with my Little One during the summer.

"Do you know what makes it rain?" he asked.

I had barely said the word "precipitation" when he started shaking his head vehemently. "No, Momma. Look!" He pointed heavenward toward a fading vapor trail. "Rockets poke holes in the clouds and let out the rain!"

I snuck a glance into the backseat, where once again, grandpa and grandson were getting loud and boisterous. A book on the heavens to correct misconceptions: $20. A trip to Disneyland with two boys (generations apart): Ouch on the pocketbook. Ouch on the ears. Ouch on the stomach from laughing at them. But learning about life from your Grandpa's knee: Priceless.

Something about concrete

For the first time in his 5-year life, my little boy woke me up before the alarm. He's as much a morning person as I am—we get up because we have to, and there certainly is no whistling or singing when the sun rises. My little boy is often groggier than I am in the morning. Often his first squeaky word is "Cof—fee." And by the way he makes opening his eyelids look difficult, he needs it...too bad I switched to decaf years ago. We both adhere to the philosophy that if people were meant to pop out of bed, we'd all sleep in toasters.

Even the excitement of opening presents Christmas morning isn't enough to make him want to rise and shine. He just doesn't do mornings. Dragging him out of bed and plopping him in front of all the glittering paper and silvery bows isn't enough to break the effects of the Sandman.

So feeling his little hands shaking my arm saying "Wake up Momma, wake up!" was quite unusual.

"What's the matter?" I asked, pulling him under the covers and snuggling him so I could go back to sleep.

"Momma, they are coming to pour *'ment* today!" he squealed, rolling out of my grasp.

Oh, yes, the cement truck was scheduled to be here at 8. I rolled over to look at the clock—5:27. "Sweetie," I cooed, "they won't be here for quite a while. Why don't we go back to sleep while we wait for them?"

He hollered something my sleeping brain couldn't register, as he scooted off the bed. I closed my eyes again and promptly fell back asleep.

Socks were suddenly shoved in my face, followed by pants, shoes and a belt. "Hurry, momma, I don't want to miss it. Daddy said I can put my hands in it!" I tried hard to keep my eyes closed, but he was too enthusiastic. I groaned as I slid out of my warm covers. There is no snooze button on a child excited about pouring cement.

In a society of fast food, instant potatoes and digital cameras, it is really hard for a 5-year-old to wait hours for a concrete truck—makes a watched pot seem to boil rapidly. But eventually they arrived...as did everyone else. People came out of the woodwork to watch the concrete project. Oddly though; no one had watched the forms be built, the rebar put in place, or any other part of the shop project...but when it was time for cement, there were bystanders aplenty.

I started thinking back to my childhood. There are pictures of nearly every concrete pad my dad ever poured... but I bet he'd be hard pressed to come up with pictures from even half of our birthdays—maybe we should have "poured" our cakes to generate more interest? Soon we were pouring in the rain and attempting to hang tarps to prevent pock marks. Even the rain didn't seem to deter people. It seemed to add to the adventure.

And soon I was taking pictures too...there's just something about concrete. It's almost as much fun as bubble wrap...and requires about the same amount of self-control to keep your hands out of it. Combine that with the effects of energizing my 5-year-old, I'm thinking we need to skip the coffee and go straight for the "*'ment*!"

Life & Death

Old farmers never die:

they just go to seed.
they just get plowed under.
they just smell that way.

First contact: yesterday, today, tomorrow

*N*ovember, 1996. I was 17 years old, and shivering in my driveway. The autumn air was crisp, but I barely noticed. A brown Ford Falcon pulled into the yard, and a tall, blonde, blue-eyed boy stepped out. My teeth were starting to chatter now, and my stomach was quaking. I'm sure he said hello as I walked to his car, but the butterflies swarming my stomach were too loud to hear much.

Every inch the gentleman, he walked around and opened the car door for me and I managed a tiny wave at my dad (who was standing in the doorway of the shop watching the entire affair) before slipping into the passenger seat. My hands were shaking so bad I could barely buckle the seat belt. It seemed to take an eternity for Ryan, my 17-year-old escort, to walk back to his side of the car and get in. I was so nervous, I could barely make conversation as we pulled out of the driveway and onto the road.

An observer might have thought it common first-date jitters. But they would have been wrong. The boy sitting across from me in the orange glow of dash lights, was my best friend in the entire world. My apprehension actually stemmed from our destination—the movie theater—the one place in town my parents didn't allow me to frequent. And I was sneaking out to watch Star Trek: First Contact. Ryan and I shared a passion of science fiction, and with minimal coaxing , I had agreed to tell my dad we were "going for ice cream." As fate would have it, the movie theater was filled with friends of my dad's. I thought I was going to die. His eyes teased me, but he never said a word when I covered my head with his jacket as the credits rolled and those friends began filing past us.

The last 20 years of my life is peppered with bizarre memories like eating grapefruit and black coffee (his favorite meal), brushing our teeth from a shared mug of water amidst the mud huts of Africa and spending hours under the hood of a car talking anything but sports (a mutually hated subject). We borrowed books, swapped stories and shared dreams. He wanted to work on classic cars and race boats. He made those dreams reality. He eventually built himself a hot rod metal fabrication shop near Seattle, and I was so proud as his cars began covering the fronts of many hot rod magazines.

He recently turned 32, and I picked up a birthday card, wrote in it, and promptly set it on my table. I'd mail it "tomorrow." This last Saturday, during a sanctioned boat race in Olympia, he died. And his birthday card still sits on my table. A terrible reminder that there are no "tomorrows" only "todays." To my best friend, Ryan Butler, thank you for those beautiful memories of yesterday…may you Race In Peace.

Carpe diem

I swished my red toenails into the carpet as I listened to all the nice things people were saying about my old Sabbath School teacher. "What a great cook she was," followed by "She was so family oriented," and "She never passed up a good hot springs." As I listened, I wondered if she knew the impact she'd had in these peoples' lives.

Funerals are very introspective, and I thought back to my own life. Did I ever tell my dad how much his little "Roses are Red…" poems in my yogi bear lunch box meant to me? Or how much I always appreciated those late night talks with my grandma, after my grandpa went to bed? Does my brother know how much I enjoy trying goofy things with him—like snowboarding behind a snowmobile? With memories still swirling around my brain ushers began filing us past the casket, and carpe diem suddenly took on a new meaning.

We need to live like our warranty expired yesterday. Seize the moments; tell your loved ones what makes them special to you. Memorial Day is coming up, and while I realize this is a time to honor your lost friends and family, I challenge you to carpe diem; tell your loved ones how much they mean to you and why. Life isn't about what you know; it's about who you know—and how well you loved them.

Vegetable death

*I*t's summer time…a time of garden fresh green beans, tomatoes, zucchini, carrots, eggplant, and my husband has come down with a severe case of vegetablitis. Being vegetarian, one would surmise that he would relish this time of sunshine and eating out of the garden…but it turns out he leans more toward the 'tarian' than the 'vege.'

He picks out the chunks of tomatoes in stew or chili…he's afraid tomatoes cause cancer. Onions get picked out of his sandwiches as he reminds me that onions cause tumors. He can't eat mushrooms, athletes foot you know. Peppers make you sneeze, and he doesn't want to take the chance with zucchini—they might cause stones. He also wants to watch his eggplant intake, after all too much dairy is bad for your health.

After posting his eating disorder in a status update on facebook, one comment told him how grateful he should be that okra didn't grow in this neck of the woods. What kind of health problems might okra cause, I inquired. My uncle responded with a one word answer, "death."

Well, I guess that just about sums it up…vegetables can be healthy…but if you eat them, you will die. Of course, if you don't eat them you'll still die… I guess vegetablitis can be deadly after all!

A nap, a vacation, & a fly

"There was an old woman who swallowed a fly. I don't know why she swallowed that fly…"

Every school child has learned the words to the silly song. I was no exception. Although, I never gave the lyrics much thought…that is until last weekend.

There I was, on vacation at the Pacific Coast. Blue sky, no fog, a hot cup of cocoa, and astonishingly my little boy fell sound asleep on the couch. With nothing else needing my attention—other than a great who-done-it next to the bed—I relished in the idea of a rare and unexpected nap.

I snuggled into the down comforter and pulled a green blanket up around my chin. My eyelids dropped weightily as my head touched the pillow.

Soon I was dreamily exploring the remnants of the Titanic, swimming down the main staircase, and gently poking my head into sediment-filled staterooms. As I kicked my fins into the swimming pool, I noticed a bubbling leak in mask. I twisted the mask around, trying to get a better seal.

But instead of sealing, my movements had made it worse, and now the bubbles were swarming around my eyes and nose. I tilted my head back, and pressed my hand against the top of my mask, attempting to clear the water.

Before I could make any miraculous discoveries on board the legendary ship, the bubbles began to buzz, and I suddenly awoke to a lone fly skitting across my face.

I waved my hand across my face, but was reluctant to move, still enjoying the blissful state of drowsiness. The fly left, and I quickly floated to the tractor. I was in a huge straw field, and I only had one more row left to bale, what a great feeling.

My dog could sense my elation too, and began wiggling. "Almost done," I told her, patting her head. That's when the bolt sheared. At first, my dog entertained herself eating mice and chasing rabbits, but cleaning out a big baler isn't fast, and soon she was sticking her nose in my eyes, cheeks, and forehead. When her cold wet nose stuck in my ear, I gave her a good swat—and realized I was chasing the same pesky fly.

By now, my entire body was in the dredges of sleep, and I couldn't muster up much more of a defensive response than pulling the blanket over my head. That worked a few minutes—until the fly found a tiny hole, and soon it was buzzing under the covers. I was quickly losing my rare opportunity to take a nap. I could feel my blood pressure rising. There was a whole trailer to fly about....why did it need to use my personal airspace? Too soon, I heard the little patter of feet... I sat up, glaring at the fly as he ducked for cover.

And that's when I had my epiphany. The Old Woman in the song, was probably the same Old Woman who lived in the shoe with a passel of children. One afternoon all her children fell asleep at the same time...and she laid down for a much-deserved nap...and now you know why she swallowed that fly....

Life, death and sexting

My eyes burned. I held them shut for a few seconds, then tried to focus on my empty word processor screen. Reducing someone's life to 500 words seems disrespectful. Which stories to tell and which to leave out? Jim Eardley was an interesting storyteller, and sharing an office with him for over 7 years, I have been blessed to hear many.

Do I tell about when he and his wife met and went out on an awkward blind date, where he was told she thought him Clark Gable and she being told he thought her Vivian Leigh? Needless to say, they weren't quite as impressed with each other as their friends had led them to believe... but about 8 months later, they tried a second date....not as Rhett and Scarlet, just Jim and Barbra, with much better results.

Or do I tell about their honeymoon, where they borrowed his sister's car, headed to Vegas, and picked up a hitch-hiker. Or maybe when his son was 2, and they couldn't get him to sleep. Finally at wit's end, Jim told him "Fine, you wanna watch TV....watch TV." Jim got up around 2 to check on him, and he found the little guy, still wide awake, sitting in his rocker watching the snow on the television... Jim left him there.

Or when a lady at the store pulled out his baby's pacifier, and gave him a lecture on the dangers of binkies.

Or maybe the time when Jim got pulled over for speeding, and found the officer so polite, he wrote the police station a letter with much praise for the particular officer (it should be noted here, that Jim did NOT get off, he received a ticket, he just felt the officer had been very polite). A year or so later, Jim received a phone call from his brother, who had just been pulled over by the same police officer. Upon receiving his license, the cop asked if he was related to a Mr. James Eardley.

He nodded hesitantly, and told the cop it was his brother. The cop then, told him about the letter Jim had sent. He ripped up the ticket saying to "give that brother of yours a kiss….he kept you out of a ticket."

There are so many bizarre stories that Jim has shared of his life, how to tell just one, or two. The more I thought about it, the more I cried. Who was going to call me "magician" at work as I juggled headlines and ads around on the page. Or laugh and say "whatever fits, we print." Who will cut up old newspapers on the floor with my little boy?

We have shared so much, I can't imagine going back to work at an office void of such a special man. "Oh God," I thought, "how can I do this…I don't think I can ever smile again."

At that exact moment there was a knock on the door. I rubbed my sleeve across my puffy eyes. The knock came again. I grabbed another wad of tissues and still sniffling, opened the door. It was an elderly gentleman wearing a checkered vest, cabby hat and leaning on a cane. He was hunched over, and I figured him to be in this 80s. With surprising speed, he whipped out a Bible.

The small Bible shook as he flipped through the silvery pages, but his voice was strong as he read about the pleasure of intimacy in marriage. And in a grandfatherly voice, began to tell me 10 things the Bible says about sex: everything from birth control to sexting.

I didn't know which was worse: 1. The visit, 2. the topic, or 3. the fact that it was delivered by a man in his 80s.

The dichotomy between the Norman Rockwell man and the subject matter was unbelievable. I could feel a tug of a smile.

When he finally handed me the religious tracts, and hobbled off my porch, it was a full-blown grin. 15 minutes before, I would have thought it impossible to feel amused on such a bleak day. But God knew what he was doing when he sent those Jehovah's Witnesses to my door. It was exactly what I needed….a sex talk by an old man.

I could only imagine telling this story to Jim, he would have laughed so hard, I can almost see the tears rolling down his cheeks…just as tears were rolling down mine now…only this time they were tears of memory and love.

Jim would want me to laugh, and I am sure that now whenever I see men in ties walking down the street carrying a Bible, I will smile, and think of Jim…and birth control…

Don't forget to laugh

*W*hen life gets rough, and there doesn't seem to be enough tissue's to wipe away our tears, my grandma Betty was always uplifting family and friends with her poems. Shortly before she lost her battle with cancer, she received a standing ovation from the other patients at the cancer center as she recited one of her last poems.

Don't Forget to Laugh
By Betty Rayl

When your dimples turn to wrinkles
and your hair has turned to gray
and you feel like Rip Van Winkle
when you rise to face the day.
Then you sometimes start to thinkin'
'bout the things you've learned in life
'cause the years ahead are shrinkin'
filled with happiness or strife.
There are lots of troubles
that can plague the human race,
but those will burst like bubbles
with a smile upon your face.
You never see the shadows
when you're looking at the sun
and dark depression never grows
when you're bent on having fun.
So when the race is over,
and they write your epitaph
be sure that they remember,
you did not forget to laugh.

Our little Steam Tractor

"*T*hat man didn't take a very good picture," my 4-year-old said, looking at the ultrasound picture of our newest addition to the family. I had to laugh, looking at the grainy photo of black spots and white lumps that was supposedly a tiny baby. "It may not be a great photo, but it was definitely the most expensive photo shoot I've ever paid for," my husband declared.

I had just entered my second trimester, and we thought we'd wait just a bit longer to announce our news, so we had a long talk with our 4-year-old telling him he had to keep it secret. He reluctantly agreed, but it didn't stop him and his imaginary friend from creating names on his chalkboard for "his little girl." The name they finally decided on was Steam Tractor.

As my belly began to grow, so did our plans for the future. Would we add on to the house? Would we need an extra buddy seat in the swather? Our only-child status would expire on July 6. My husband began planning out the hay cutting schedule to accommodate, and I designed the baby announcement. Excitement abounded. We just had to wait for the right time to share the news. But, like most babies, they play on their own schedule, with little regard to the calendar of the parents. I started having a few health problems, and we decided to tell our immediate families and elicit prayers.

I was on the phone with my grandma, when my little boy overheard me telling "our secret." He was cross with me to the point of tears until he realized that meant he got to tell his Nanny (my mom). His face lit up as he told her all about his little baby sister.

He was adamant he didn't want a brother, "I won't play with a boy!" he declared, "but I'll show a girl all our lambs, and take her for rides on my four-wheeler…and we can buy her pink rubber boots…and a pair for me too!"

They say God laughs when we plan in pen; and our erasers were in high gear as my health continued to decline. We had been busy with plans: plans for our upcoming vacation, plans for names, sleeping arrangements, and even a side-by-side to accommodate the entire family at the sand dunes. Soon I was on bed rest, and our tickets to Ireland had to be refunded. But the baby was okay, so we continued to pray.

All that changed late one Tuesday night. We read bedtime stories to our little boy, then snuggled into our warm down covers. Contractions soon interrupted our sleep, and 6 hours later my husband and I sobbed in each other's arms, a miniature baby beside us—pink and lifeless. Our plans, our dreams, lost in the blood and the tears.

Life goes right, life goes wrong; life goes on. My little boy, doing his best to cheer us up, came and offered me a big hug. "I love you, Momma," he whispered, "and when that little girl comes, I'll tell her to give you a big hug too!"

Tears squeezed beneath my lashes as I pressed my damp face into his little neck. The hardest lesson in life is saying good-bye to those we love, and it is no less hard with a tiny babe we never met. Time and tears will dull the pain, but we will always remember our little "Steam Tractor"—the joy, laughter, and hope you brought us—regardless of how bad your "photo" was.

Life is like a camera

*W*hat are we but our stories? And I have been so honored by the personal stories my readers have shared with me following the weeks of saying goodbye to our Little Steam Tractor.

Pain is never desired, and the loss of our unborn baby has been agonizing...but the stories and notes my readers sent to me have been healing. Thank you.

I wasn't alone in this, and the connectivity of support from you all has been a blessing. I read stories of sorrow and guilt and of an unquenchable sadness. And while most of the stories made me cry, they also suggested hope: hope for the future, and hope for a life better than this one.

Just like everything else in life, this was a moment of growth...a moment when life hit a wall. We we learned that with the right help, we could climb it. And for just a moment, before we dropped to the other side, we stood on top, amidst the love from our friends and community and felt that all would be well again.

Support came in all shapes and sizes: plants, cards, emails, and even a tub of my favorite cherry chip frosting. But one of the notes that really resonated came from my sister.

Knowing my photography addiction, her message fit well,

it read:

Life is like a camera, just focus on what's important, and capture the good times. Develop from the negatives, and if things don't turn out, just take another shot.

Made in the USA
Lexington, KY
12 June 2017